"Through honest assessment and stories, *Can We Trust AI?* this fascinating and controver: renowned scientist and invento research, development, and ap| While he's immersed in its complexities, his book provides an accessible entrée to the subject for readers of all backgrounds who wish to learn more about its advantages, capabilities, and potential dangers."

"A first-class tour through the evolution, promise and perils of AI by one of its leading lights. A great book for cutting through both the hype and the fear-mongering surrounding AI."

"Artificial intelligence in the past and present; in research labs and industry; in everyday lives and war zones; in reality and science fiction. By going back and forth, Chellappa challenges us to think about what AI truly means to the world, now and into the future. A must-read book for everyone from early adopters of these technologies to their skeptics."

"Rama Chellappa's work on automatic recognition of humans has helped define AI research for four decades. In this book, he carefully addresses the history and future of AI, its compelling applications, including in medicine and autonomous driving, and its ethical challenges, questionable uses, potential biases, and privacy issues. It's a terrific and highly personal read!"

—Alan Bovik, PhD, Professor, Electrical and Computer Engineering, University of Texas at Austin; recipient of the 2021 Technology and Engineering Emmy® Award from the National Academy of Television Arts and Sciences and the 2022 IEEE Edison Medal

"Having made notable contributions to the field throughout his career, Dr. Chellappa is well positioned to predict what AI is capable of and to recognize its current limitations. In this easy-to-follow and insightful book, he weaves together a cautiously optimistic recounting of pioneering advances in AI with a frank reckoning of its potential shortcomings, along with suggestions for improvements, including greater diversity in academic programs and hiring in the field."

—Maya Kabkab, PhD, Staff Software Engineer, Waymo LLC

"Can we trust AI? Are we safer turning the wheel over to our AI driver than we are driving ourselves? Do face recognition systems strengthen or weaken our society? Rama Chellappa, a renowned researcher in AI and computer vision, has written a delightfully personalized and insightful book that rationally addresses these questions and provides the reader with important historical context on the development of AI over the past half-century. A valuable read for anyone interested in how AI will shape our future."

—Larry Davis, PhD, Professor Emeritus, Computer Science; Director of the Center for Automation Research (CfAR), University of Maryland, College Park

"Chellappa provides a wonderful journey through artificial intelligence's origins and experiments, and explains how its advances impact the world we're living in today. He shares his expertise on the intricacies of AI technologies and applications in a simple yet effective way."

—Rajeev Ranjan, PhD, Senior Applied Scientist, Amazon One

"Grounded in Dr. Chellappa's decades of experience working in the field of artificial intelligence, *Can We Trust AI?* provides an excellent overview of how these technologies have evolved over the past five decades and offers a realistic opinion on current capabilities. The narrative also addresses several key issues with current AI systems, including bias concerns and the lack of appropriate regulations to prevent their misuse."

—Raviteja Vemulapalli, PhD, Senior Research Scientist, Google LLC

Can We Trust AI?

Can We Trust AI?

RAMA CHELLAPPA, PhD

With Eric Niiler

Johns Hopkins University Press
Baltimore

Johns Hopkins Wavelengths is a registered trademark of the Johns Hopkins University

© 2022 Rama Chellappa
All rights reserved. Published 2022
Printed in the United States of America on acid-free paper
9 8 7 6 5 4 3 2 1

Johns Hopkins University Press
2715 North Charles Street
Baltimore, Maryland 21218
www.press.jhu.edu

Cataloging-in-Publication Data is available from the Library of Congress.

A catalog record for this book is available from the British Library.

ISBN: 978-1-4214-4530-4 (paperback)
ISBN: 978-1-4214-4531-1 (ebook)
ISBN: 978-1-4214-4532-8 (ebook, open access)

Special discounts are available for bulk purchases of this book.
For more information, please contact Special Sales at specialsales@jh.edu.

Contents

Preface

I'VE BEEN CURIOUS about how technology works since my childhood in Chennai, India, in the 1960s. During that era, America was a vibrant hub of innovation, so when I was 10 years old, a friend encouraged me to write to the US embassy in New Delhi, expressing my interest in learning about the United States. I wrote the letter in my native language, Tamil, and addressed it simply to "Ambassador, US Embassy, New Delhi, India." To my delight, two months later I received a beautiful book with President George Washington on the cover. I read the book, which detailed the nation's history, people, system of government, and contributions to science and technology, from cover to cover.

The book (and the gesture) deepened my interest in both technological advances and the United States. So naturally, like so many children and adults around the world, I listened to the 1969 moon landing on the radio in my family's home. I can still hear the distinctive Quindar tones that punctuated the conversations between the Apollo astronauts and the NASA Mission Control Center in Houston. A few months after that remarkable event, a cousin who worked as a lecturer in the aerospace engineering department at a local college took me to the US consulate in Chennai to watch a State Department film about the moon landing. The film further fueled my interest in technology and computers, and it strengthened my resolve to find a way to travel to the United States to study both subjects.

As a first step on this path, I became a member of the American library at the consulate, visiting every two weeks to borrow a book. Although I loved cricket, I was a bookworm and excelled in mathematics and statistics. As a teenager, I invited neighborhood kids and classmates over to our modest apartment each semester to help them with homework and prepare for exams, drawing math equations on my bedroom door as if it were a chalk board—a foreshadowing of my teaching career. My father began his career as a high school teacher and a few years later joined the Reserve Bank of India so that he could better support our family. He always talked about how much he enjoyed his tenure as a teacher, and this motivated me to be an academician, albeit on a bigger playing field. By 1975, as I was finishing my undergraduate degree in engineering at the University of Madras, I told my parents that one day I would leave India and become a professor in the United States.

I guess that early interest in mentoring my neighbors paid off. Since my first stint as a professor at the University of Southern California (USC) in the early 1980s, I've advised 114 doctoral students' dissertations. Former students of mine are the heads of four university departments, and others work on research teams at Google, Amazon, Apple, and Facebook.

When people ask me, "So, what is it that you do?" I say, "I groom future researchers." I don't say that I publish papers or help invent technologies. I've always valued the idea of helping others, from scribbling those equations on the bedroom door to helping my students flourish in academic and global business enterprises, and finding ways that artificial intelligence can make our lives safe and better.

GLIMMERS OF AI

I first heard the term *artificial intelligence* as a graduate student way back in 1978. I had just come to the United States after completing my master's degree at the Indian Institute of Science (IISc) in Bangalore (now called Bengaluru) to pursue a doctorate in electrical engineering at Purdue University in Indiana. The IISc is the premier research university in India and boasts of having had the Noble laureate Sir C. V. Raman (who first published observations on the change in the wavelength of light that occurs when a light beam is deflected by molecules—henceforth called the Raman effect) on its faculty and as its director. The city of Bengaluru has become a vital hub of high-tech industries in software and information technologies, communications, and the aerospace sector. During my time there, though, artificial intelligence was considered a subfield of computer science—a way for a computer to follow a series of instructions, or an algorithm, to solve problems and to "think" on its own. It was mainly a theoretical concept associated with nascent programs that played games rather than a functioning piece of software that could run a machine, car, or robot. Computer scientists who worked on AI in the 1960s and '70s dreamed of having their programs beat a human chess champion (which finally happened in 1996),[1] automatically translate Russian documents, or solve complex mathematical puzzles and theorems. At Purdue, I began working on pattern recognition and image processing, which led to a career path combining artificial intelligence with sensors, cameras, and microphones that would ultimately allow a computer to "see."

Today, pattern recognition enables computers to search through enormous sets of data to connect the dots on otherwise impossible-to-perceive patterns that could be useful in real-world applications, perhaps in identifying images of people and objects or understanding voice instructions. These tasks are now commonplace. Just think of Apple's Siri or Amazon's Alexa personal assistants, Google's Translate app, or even the ubiquitous automated speed cameras that capture the license plate number from a fast-moving car. During my years as a graduate student, these applications existed only as science fiction. With my colleagues at Purdue, I worked on a rudimentary system that would recognize individual sounds from words spoken on a recording device and then feed them into a computer, a field called speech recognition. Engineers and computer scientists at IBM, Carnegie Mellon University, and Bell Labs were advancing the same field in the 1970s. Purdue's electrical engineering department boasted of having some of the world's premier researchers in pattern recognition, image processing, and computer vision; those heralded professors included King-Sun Fu, Ken Fukunaga, R. L. Kashyap, and Thomas Huang.

Professor Fu, a leading scholar in statistical and syntactic pattern recognition, was the instructor for my AI course in the spring of 1978. We used the only book available at the time, *Problem-Solving Methods in AI*, by the pioneer Nils Nilsson. I also took a course taught by Professor Fukunaga called Introduction to AI that barely mentioned neural networks in the first lecture; today, neural networks dominate the fields of artificial intelligence, machine learning, and data science. As graduate students in engineering, our focus was on the mathematics, statistics, and computer language tools that would make artificial intelligence work. We didn't debate the ethics of AI and privacy, fears of superintelligent machines replacing humans, or even the benefits of artificial "friends" helping out in hospitals, schools, or emergency rescues. We were thinking only about writing our papers and getting good grades—getting things right while devoting our free time to imagining the possibilities. I remember going to a conference in Chicago in 1978, where I worked as a student volunteer setting up slide projectors at sessions on pattern recognition and image processing. One session dealt with speech recognition, which was a big focus of AI then and still is today. Raj Reddy of Carnegie Mellon University gave a talk about the speech recognition system he was designing for chess, so that someone could speak commands for each move and the computer would understand the risks and how to respond. I was amazed by his talk and the idea that a computer could understand what a person said, which inspired me to delve further into this promising world of AI in bits and pieces.

Over time, as I began my academic career as a professor at USC and then at the University of Maryland, I found a niche in AI in the field of computer vision, which is developing the tools to enable a computer or robot to see its surroundings. I realized that developing a way to make computers interact with the world through cameras and other sensors such as microphones would be a big advancement in understanding their environment. Getting a computer to see was the first step; it also required the intelligence to know *why* it needs to see, what action to take, and what the consequences are of sensing the world around it. That's how computer vision and artificial intelligence come together.

VISION PLUS AI

Azriel Rosenfeld, a pioneering computer scientist at the University of Maryland, opened my eyes to what might lie ahead in the fields of pattern recognition and computer vision, and he would become my first true mentor. I'd worked in his lab as a graduate student during the spring of 1979, before returning to Purdue to complete my doctoral work. Having had such an amazing experience, I visited Rosenfeld's lab again during winter and summer breaks and worked with him on building image representations using Markov random field (MRF) models, an important part of the AI toolbelt that interprets data represented as mathematical graphs.

Rosenfeld served as an external reviewer on my doctoral dissertation on developing models of processing and analyzing images by factoring in uncertainty and unpredictability, known as stochastic models. I published most of my dissertation as a series of technical reports released by the computer vision laboratory at University of Maryland, which Azriel directed. While he wasn't sure whether MRFs were appropriate as representations for images and videos due to their linear structure, he nevertheless encouraged my efforts.

Rosenfeld also played a major role in starting the Image Understanding Program at the Defense Advanced Research Projects Agency (DARPA). In the early 1980s, he was one of the first in the field to discuss the possibility of outfitting vehicles with cameras so they could move on their own. This line of research, combining AI, remotely operated vehicles, and vehicle-mounted digital video cameras, culminated in the $1 million DARPA Grand Challenge in 2004. The contest pitted teams of engineers to build and operate autonomous vehicles to navigate a 142-mile course that ran across the California-Nevada desert and fueled the development of a new class of autonomous trucks that could ultimately replace humans in hazardous military operations, such as supply convoys. Although none of the vehicles finished the course in the first of several such DARPA events, this early test spurred a cycle of trial-and-error technology development in university labs and start-up companies that over time has gotten us closer than ever to a world of driverless taxis and robot-operated cargo trucks. (For more on the DARPA challenge, see pages 106–7, 112-13.)

AI'S GROWTH SPURT

When I was in graduate school at Purdue, AI was in the midst of a federal-funding "winter" when research dollars were frozen. These cutbacks happened for several reasons: DARPA switched funding from basic AI research into more applied military-related projects; the United Kingdom stopped funding AI research because of a lack of results (documented in a 1973 report by British mathematician James Lighthill); and a general skepticism had crept in about computers' capability of performing the tasks required by artificial intelligence. There's been a significant thaw since those days; now, both the federal government and private technology firms are pouring billions of dollars into the field. US government spending on AI topped $1 billion in 2020,[2] while the global marketplace for AI enterprises is predicted to exceed $228 billion by 2026.[3] Today, most universities offer undergraduate courses or even degrees in artificial intelligence; *U.S. News & World Report* ranks these programs just as they do academic departments in business, engineering, medicine, and liberal arts.[4] Artificial intelligence technologies are being studied everywhere, not just as an academic pursuit in labs like mine but also in hundreds of start-up companies, massive technology campuses in Silicon Valley, Boston, Pittsburgh, Washington State, and Texas, and even in high school summer camps.

My colleagues and students at Johns Hopkins—and previously at the University of Maryland—and I have been working more recently on developing facial recognition programs that allow computers to process video images from long distances—programs that might identify who is on the deck of a boat or sitting several hundred yards away in a café.

These programs can help identify lawbreakers, terrorists, or even unruly fans at a soccer match. But the same image recognition systems are also being used in medicine to help doctors and radiologists spot tumors, blockages, and other tissue abnormalities more quickly and accurately than manual scans. Facial recognition, deep learning, and computer vision, combined with new kinds of sensor and computer processing abilities, are also key to ensuring that automated vehicles navigate their environments safely. AI algorithms have helped epidemiologists track the coronavirus pandemic and develop vaccines. AI has also changed the way we connect with family and friends, find our political and social tribes, apply for jobs, and maybe even select a partner through online matching apps. While we may not be ready to turn over the keys to a robot driver, AI-powered automated systems are learning quickly and helping take the burden off human drivers while also improving safety through new and widely available intelligent vehicles, using AI to navigate and detect hazards before the driver can react, with tools such as lane detection and alerts for vehicles approaching blind spots.

During the past decade, AI has migrated from university research centers to the cubicles and boardrooms of Silicon Valley tech giants and onto our mobile phones and laptops. It's become like oxygen: It's everywhere around us, although not always visible, and we're increasingly dependent on it. As artificial intelligence technologies transform our society, the need to consider the ethics of what these AI algorithms are doing—how accurate they are and how they affect real people—is increasingly critical. There's growing concern about biases in some facial recognition programs that are less accurate in identifying darker-skinned faces. In addition, some voice recognition systems have struggled to understand, and thus take commands from, female voices. Deepfake images and videos can trick the brain into thinking something happened that really didn't, or create a person who doesn't exist through an online identity. Part of my current research is focused on how to detect those deepfakes and stop them from spreading.

Although I'd been working with AI and its applications for several decades, I got a direct sense of its immense power to impact society in 2017 while working on a facial recognition project called Janus along with a team of researchers from several academic computer science labs. The goal was to design a system that could recognize identities from short clips of real-world video rather than front-facing still images, and to engineer it so that its accuracy would improve over time. Just the fact that we were able to build an end-to-end system that performed beyond anything I ever imagined, and that is now in operational use, convinced me that AI has already made a significant impact on all our lives. The facial recognition program my students and research associates helped design went from our lab to the federal government, where it is now being used to improve security and identify lawbreakers.

Imagine today's AI as a toddler who needs constant supervision as well as constant care and feeding. Some people worry about what happens when it becomes a teenager and rebels against its parents. But it's at this point that the comparison between AI and humans breaks down. We're training AI agents to do the tasks that we don't want to do, or that are too dangerous for us—not to replace us. The technology's strength is in completing narrow-focus tasks, such as searching images, detecting movement, or assembling patterns from vast amounts of data. Artificial intelligence agents still can't think for themselves, exercise judgment or true "intelligence" about their decision-making capabilities, or create other AI agents like themselves. Nor should we want them to.

MAKING AI MORE EQUITABLE

AI and its components—deep learning, reasoning, computer vision's facial and action recognition (a term that describes a subject's movement pattern)—must continue to evolve in order to become more accurate and effective. In the coming chapters, we'll explore how AI has developed since its beginnings in the post–World War II era to today's AI-driven facial recognition, smart cars systems, and programs that help doctors diagnose illness. We'll also examine some of the growing concerns about AI and its weaknesses when it comes to identifying individuals, especially those from communities of color. Just as we learn more fully when exposed to diverse sources and human experiences, so, too, AI algorithms should be trained on larger and more diverse sets of images and words in order to perform accurately. Even if we decide that AI agents don't belong in our homes, we may value them as partners at work or in public. These decisions have to be made by bringing AI technology developers, ethicists, and regulators together so that a proper balance between technological advances and societal interests can be maintained.

As AI-based systems become ubiquitous, their vulnerabilities to adversarial cyberattacks cause growing concerns about their effectiveness and the risk for users. Although I believe that the widespread use of AI-based technologies will have a net positive impact on society, they're also being used to create misinformation on various social platforms and media. Ongoing efforts to detect and mitigate these malicious infiltrations of systems and misinformation that are distributed through various media formats are also topics for further exploration.

On the other hand, there are numerous exciting avenues for AI to evolve into a vital vehicle for improving human resilience and development, including the role it can play in eldercare and helping improve accessibility for people who suffer from poor vision or hearing loss—or even who are completely blind or deaf. Finally, AI can play a significant role in personalized education that may benefit students from different backgrounds and those who have disabilities and learning challenges.

Artificial intelligence's amalgamation of engineering, math, and statistics helps machines make autonomous decisions, and it's here to stay. Its applications are broad and deep throughout societies around the globe, and they're expanding each day to become ever more deeply ingrained in our lives. We may not soon encounter cyborgs or the superintelligent AI-powered robots of Philip K. Dick's novella *Minority Report* (and its subsequent film adaptation), but we're seeing elements of AI agents being used throughout all levels of society. After four decades of closely studying, experimenting, monitoring, and reporting on the development of AI, I'm now a Bloomberg Distinguished Professor in electrical and computer engineering and biomedical engineering at the Whiting School of Engineering at Johns Hopkins. It's been an exciting ride that's about to take promising new directions. I'm eager to share what I've learned about what artificial intelligence is, how to guide its development, and how to harness it to make life safer, better, and more interesting for all of us.

Can We Trust AI?

CHAPTER 1

The Birth and Growth of AI

OF THE MANY DIVERSE TECHNOLOGIES that have changed our world in the past century, artificial intelligence may be the most influential. It's become so without many of us knowing it, a stealthy presence seeping into our lives like an electronic ghost with a super brain. In the past two decades, AI has evolved from an academic research tool taught to graduate students alongside mathematics and statistics to a driver of today's commerce, social media, policing, health care, and transportation. The combination of advanced algorithms, powerful computers (together with the capacity to store their enormous volumes of data), and advances in sensor technology is altering everything from weather forecasting to weapons systems, from cancer detection to finance. AI has become a tool for societal good, helping humans make decisions more quickly and accurately. The tools of artificial intelligence have also spawned a massive commercial industry that expands in both the reach and the variety of applications each year.

What is artificial intelligence? You'll get many different

answers if you don't ask an expert. Some people's understanding of the science is centered on their immediate experiences with the technology, and they often cite the example of a digital personal assistant like Amazon's Alexa or Apple's Siri, a disembodied voice that gives directions, plays music, or offers a quick summary of the day's weather. Science fiction fans might talk about the futuristic AI-driven robots in films that are portrayed as helpful and cute like R2D2 in *Star Wars,* malevolent like the Terminator, or mind-bending like the agents in *The Matrix.* But artificial intelligence is both much more complex than its uses in household appliances and at a much simpler stage of development than what Hollywood has portrayed. It's more at the intellectual level of a curious toddler than a silver-haired genius planning world domination.

The current form of AI is relatively narrow. It can effectively complete specific tasks that it's been programmed for: tag photos, play board games, scan résumés, select potential partners on online dating sites, or pick the most efficient route through traffic. It also can do much more complex things like identify potential vaccine targets and classify stars. The gap between the kind of AI that's in use today and what many of us desire or read about is pretty big. Here's how Gary Marcus and Ernest Davis, authors of *Rebooting AI: Building Artificial Intelligence We Can Trust,* describe this disjunction: "We wanted Rosie the Robot, ready at a moment's notice to change our kids' diapers and whip up dinner, but what we got was Roomba, a hockey puck–shaped vacuum cleaner with wheels."[1] In fact, some experts view current artificial intelligence technology as equivalent only to a newborn. One of them is Charles Isbell, dean and professor of computing at Georgia Institute of Technology and director of the Laboratory for Interactive Artificial Intelligence. His research centers on building autonomous agents that must live and interact with large numbers of other intelligent agents, some of which may be human.

Isbell notes that while babies learn to communicate with their parents almost immediately and begin talking a few years after birth, learning complex communication like reading and writing takes a decade or more. For an AI agent to learn such skills, it, too, will need artificial parents that can nurture and guide its development. "One of the reasons that AI is so young is that we don't have that sort of natural infrastructure in place to raise it," Isbell says. "We need an AI nursery, we need AI parents, we need an AI family. We don't have any of those things."[2]

As for an equivalent human age, Isbell puts today's AI stage of development at about six months. He notes that some AI programs act much "older" when they're trained to do specific tasks, such as sorting through data or images. But when asked to make complex decisions that require context, judgment, and planning for unexpected scenarios as humans do every waking minute? That won't happen anytime soon. "Why would we think that we can build an artificial intelligence in the space of 18 hours on a particularly narrow problem in order to be as generally intelligent as human beings?" Isbell asks. The future of AI looks promising, but its upward trajectory is unpredictable. In the short term, humans and AI will work better together as a team than either one on its own. That applies for tasks ranging from playing chess to rescuing earthquake victims. "We're going to see incredibly useful AI that will be very, very smart and help people to be better at specific things," Isbell says.

AI ON LAND, UNDER WATER, AND IN SPACE

On roads, at sea, and in orbit, artificial intelligence is helping human-built vehicles navigate, complete tasks, and avoid crashes. AI-driven tugboats are parking supertankers in Singapore, while AI captains are steering Israeli car-carriers across the Mediterranean and piloting bulk coal and grain carriers along Ohio's Cuyahoga River.[3] AI-captained ships can be safer because the pilots don't fall asleep after sailing all night; they can also be programmed to use less fuel to reach port and unload cargo seamlessly.

Rovers are equipped with AI programs by engineers at the National Aeronautics and Space Administration (NASA), allowing them to navigate and explore Mars.[4] Oceanographers are deploying similar AI navigation programs to steer deep-sea vehicles as they explore miles-deep underwater volcanoes and hot springs,[5] and help collect climate indicator data. As the world's oceans become more crowded with resource developments such as off-shore wind farms, aquaculture pens, and gas pipelines, these robotic vehicles are becoming common industrial inspection tools that check for signs of trouble. Since seawater's particles and lack of light at great depths block visuals, and density impedes broadband-based underwater communications, some researchers are experimenting with new forms of sound-based communications. These acoustic sensing and communications systems, when combined with machine-learning techniques, might identify underwater objects just as well as the most intelligent ocean inhabitant, the dolphin. "We know that marine mammals can massively outperform our best sonars," says James Bellingham, executive director of the Johns Hopkins Institute for Assured Autonomy and a pioneer in the development of autonomous underwater vehicles. "They can tell the difference between different objects, small objects all the way across a swimming pool in ways we don't yet understand. Now there's this hope that maybe the tools of machine learning could get us to a place where we begin to sort of see some marine mammal–type performance in the underwater environment."

Bellingham says machine-learning algorithms can boost the perception capabilities of underwater vehicles that are lowered into the sea from oceanographic research vessels to look for shipwrecks, sunken planes, old mines, or other objects on the seafloor. By incorporating tools of artificial intelligence into the vehicle's on-board computer, the device could then process acoustic signals, identify reasonable targets, and then make decisions about where to look. All this happens within the vehicle without contacting a human controller back on the ship, kind of like an AI-powered robot dolphin. Bellingham cautions that deployment of these super-smart sea-prowling vehicles is still just over the horizon, although individual components of this scenario are within reach today. "We've been talking about doing this in the underwater field since the 1990s, it's just that the technology hasn't really supported it yet. But AI [and machine learning] starts giving you some of the perception skills that give you the confidence that maybe you could actually pull it off."[6]

From exploring deep space to understanding our changing climate, scientists collect mountains of digital data from direct measurements such as those from ocean buoys as well as from remote sensors on satellites and radio telescopes. All these data points are uploaded into cloud-based servers for researchers' mining programs to make sense of them. AI algorithms feed, grow, and learn on big datasets, because access to them means that the algorithms can train better and have their results assessed and compared for accuracy. Artificial intelligence combined with radar, sonar, and other sensors has facilitated the development of autonomous vehicles on land, in the air, and at sea. But why hasn't anyone pulled off an AI-powered passenger car?

Despite the best efforts of firms like Tesla, Google, and Uber to develop them, we still don't have a reliable self-driving car for consumers.[7] The big obstacle is that current sensor technology can be compromised by bad weather or poor lighting, especially at high speeds. But in many cities in Europe and Asia, slow-moving automated trucks, ferries, delivery vans, and shuttle buses are humming along with artificial intelligence working in tandem with the vehicles' mechanical engines. I'll explore some of these advances in greater detail in my discussion of the history and development of self-driving vehicles in chapter 4.

FLORIDA'S BIG BROTHER

As is true with most technologies, unregulated AI has a dark side as well. Some critics fear that its ability to collect and analyze large amounts of data quickly will concentrate power in governments' hands. That's what happened when a Florida sheriff decided to use AI to "predict" the likelihood of criminal behavior in a community.

In 2011 Pasco County Sheriff Chris Nocco developed a plan to cut crime in his community before it happened using cutting-edge tools of intelligence gathering, artificial intelligence, and machine learning. These were used to develop a software program designed by the sheriff's office with the help of private consultants that assembled a list of people in the county predicted to commit crimes based on arrest histories, unspecified intelligence, and arbitrary decisions by police analysts. The sheriff sent deputies to question anyone whose name appeared on the computer-generated list, often without probable cause, a search warrant, or evidence of a specific crime. The people on the list were presumed guilty until proved innocent, according to reporting by the *Tampa Bay Times*, which was awarded the Pulitzer Prize in 2021 for its coverage of the issue.[8] Despite complaints by families that had been targeted, Nocco expanded the program to include a similar predictive crime program at local schools. Families have sued the county, calling the predictive policing system unconstitutional.[9] The fate of Pasco County's predictive policing is still in the courts.

Then there's China, which rolled out a "social credit score" algorithm in 2014 that collects large amounts of data on its citizens and ranks them based on their behaviors such as bad driving, smoking in nonsmoking zones, buying too many video games, and posting fake news online, specifically about terrorist attacks or airport security. A bad score can, for example, bar people from airline flights or from buying certain luxury goods. George Orwell forecast this kind of government effort to track its citizens using big data in his 1949 dystopian novel, *1984*. The social credit system has blacklisted 10 million people and companies—firms that have ignored court orders, violated food safety or environmental laws, or failed to pay employee wages, reports *Foreign Policy* magazine.[10]

I'll examine some of the security applications of the facial recognition branch of artificial intelligence and how it can help society when the right guardrails are in place. For example, as digital cameras become sharper and the processing of data more powerful, facial recognition algorithms are identifying shoplifters and US Capitol rioters. In 2018 Maryland State Police officials used facial recognition to catch a mass shooter who didn't leave any fingerprints at the crime scene. Meanwhile, Pittsburgh-based Marinus Analytics (a start-up founded by researchers from Carnegie Mellon University's Robotics Institute in 2014) developed a machine-learning AI tool called Traffic Jam that tracked and identified several thousand victims of sex trafficking. The program searches through commercial adult services ads on various online platforms and looks for potential indicators of vulnerability such as indications of drug use or images that may be of missing children or minors.

FACIAL FLAWS

At the same time that AI tools are playing a greater role in identifying lawbreakers, researchers are discovering flaws in both how some facial recognition tools are built and the results they produce. Civic leaders in San Francisco, Seattle,

Baltimore, and a few other US cities have barred local police from using these algorithms because a number of studies show that some facial recognition programs are biased against people of color, which has led to false arrests. Amazon, Microsoft, and IBM have withdrawn or suspended their facial recognition systems in the past few years because of concerns about racial profiling, although other technology firms have helped fill the void those big companies left. Federal law enforcement officials continue to deploy facial recognition technology while studying how to make it more accurate.

In realms that range from retail shopping to social media to battlefields, artificial intelligence is now a massive industry—valued at an estimated $62.5 billion in 2020 and projected to grow 40 percent annually[11]—that's full of both hype and genuine promise, but it's also firmly entrenched. With the genie out of the proverbial bottle, it makes sense to understand how this magician works and what's at stake.

MACHINE LEARNING

Discussions of artificial intelligence often refer to computer programs based on machine learning, a branch of AI that focuses on the use of data and algorithms to imitate the way humans learn, gradually improving its accuracy.[12] Think of the algorithms that Netflix uses to help you make your next film selection: if you like *Blade Runner*, maybe you'll like another science fiction movie. If you bought a special shampoo on Amazon, it will recommend another five kinds of hair-care products. Machine learning was the basis for the success of IBM's Watson computer on *Jeopardy*; it helps car-sharing services like Uber predict rider demand; and it makes it possible for Facebook to offer suggestions in your news feed.[13] The more data available to it, the better the decision AI makes. But machine learning needs human programmers to set the parameters for the task and then improve its decision-making, either by making correct choices over time or by repeating the task until a correct answer is obtained. AI, then, is the ability to create machines that can do things that normally require human intelligence; the resulting technology can reason, learn, plan, and often make predictions that prove to be accurate.

In *Artificial Intelligence: A Modern Approach*, the University of California at Berkeley's Stuart J. Russell and Google's Peter Norvig describe AI as an "intelligent agent" that, given the right information, always makes the right decision. In their introduction, they state: "We adopt the view that intelligence is concerned mainly with rational action. Ideally, an intelligent agent takes the best possible action in a situation."[14]

THE DAWN OF AI

The concept of artificial intelligence emerged in the waning days of World War II, when Vannevar Bush, the inventor who oversaw the Manhattan Project and became the first presidential science adviser, published an essay in *The Atlantic Monthly*, "As We May Think." In early 1945, Bush predicted a digital future in which humans and machines work together to process data, made possible by "an age of cheap complex devices of great reliability." In fact, one of Bush's most discerning predictions was a hypothetical device known as a memex, a knowledge database that resembles the internet, or at least Wikipedia. Bush wrote: "Consider a future device . . . in which an individual stores all his books, records, and communications, and which is mechanized so that it may be consulted with exceeding speed and flexibility. It is an enlarged intimate supplement to his memory." Bush also put his finger on one of the secrets of AI today: It's powered by humans who write code, tag images, and interpret data. As for the details, he wrote:

> The advanced arithmetical machines of the future will be electrical in nature, and they will perform at 100 times present speeds, or more. . . . They will be controlled by a control card or film, they will select their own data and manipulate it in accordance with the instructions thus inserted, they will perform complex arithmetical computations at exceedingly high speeds, and they will record results in such form as to be readily available for distribution or for later further manipula-

tion. Such machines will have enormous appetites. One of them will take instructions and data from a whole roomful of girls armed with simple keyboard punches, and will deliver sheets of computed results every few minutes. There will always be plenty of things to compute in the detailed affairs of millions of people doing complicated things.[15]

Bush wrote this at a time when there were five people for every telephone in the United States, and some rural Americans still lacked electricity.[16] Bush—who was born in 1890—had a prescient view of today's digital world. So did Alan Turing, a British mathematician, cryptographer, and computer scientist who helped turn the tides of battle in World War II by breaking the Germans' Enigma code.

THE TURING TEST

In 1950, following his groundbreaking and enemy-undermining work against Enigma, Turing, a professor at the University of Manchester at the time, devised a test that sought to determine whether a machine possessed artificial intelligence. It became known as the Turing Test. "I propose to consider the question, 'Can machines think?'" Turing wrote in his paper "Computing Machinery and Intelligence" in the journal *Mind*.[17] Turing devised an "imitation game" involving a man, a woman, and an interrogator who would pose a series of questions to each one separately. A machine would then take the place of one of the humans and "pass" the test when the interrogator could no longer tell whether the answer was coming from a person or a machine. Turing, like Bush, was able to peer ahead to a time when machines and humans could work together, as well as to foresee the need for computer sensors that can allow a machine to "see" and "hear." Here's how Turing concluded his essay:

> We may hope that machines will eventually compete with men in all purely intellectual fields. But which are the best ones to start with? Even this is a difficult decision. Many people think that a very abstract activity, like the playing of chess, would be best. It can also be maintained that it is best to provide the machine with the best sense organs that money can buy, and then teach it to understand and speak English. This process could follow the normal teaching of a child. Things would be pointed out and named, etc. Again, I do not know what the right answer is, but I think both approaches should be tried. We can only see a short distance ahead, but we can see plenty there that needs to be done.

Turing anticipated the child-machine model for how artificial intelligence could evolve and how many computer scientists approach learning. In fact, some researchers believe that the only way for artificial intelligence to become truly "intelligent" and learn on its own will be if it has other AI agents helping it along the way. Turing's final sentence about seeing only "a short distance ahead" rings true today. The concepts that he proposed in his original paper more than 70 years ago are still subfields of current AI. An AI computer would need to possess natural language processing to communicate in English; knowledge representation to store what it knows or hears; automated reasoning to use the stored information to answer questions, draw new conclusions, and make decisions; and machine learning to adapt to new circumstances, and detect and extrapolate patterns. To become a true AI robot, a successful AI computer would also need computer vision to perceive objects as well as robotics to manipulate objects and move about, according to Russell and Norvig.[18]

The 1950s gave birth to the concept of AI. The term was first used at an eight-week summer conference at Dartmouth University in New Hampshire in 1956. The group comprised 10 computer scientists led by John McCarthy, who would go on to invent the first computer language in 1960; Marvin Minsky, who founded MIT's AI lab in the 1970s; and Nathaniel Rochester, developer of the first mass-produced scientific computer, the IBM 701, unveiled in 1952. McCarthy coined the term *artificial intelligence* in a proposal for the conference. From then, the race to build a thinking machine was on.

AI Imaginings vs. AI Realities: Robotics

Of all the dream applications for artificial intelligence, nothing captures the public's imagination quite like robots. Sci-fi novels, films, and comics have featured encounters with androids, cyborgs, and robots for more than a century in works including Fritz Lang's 1927 film *Metropolis*, Philip K. Dick's 1956 novella *The Minority Report,* and Isaac Asimov's short stories from the 1940s and '50s that are collected in *I, Robot* (it was Asimov who coined the term *robotics*). These artificial intelligence agents represent a spectrum of capabilities and intentions that inspire awe, instill fear, and sometimes just make us laugh—like Marvin the Paranoid Android introduced in Douglas Adams's *The Hitchhiker's Guide to the Galaxy* in 1978.

Even though they're built from metal and wires, these robots were conceived to appear deeply human. In *Star Trek: The Next Generation,* the android character Lt. Commander Data (created by legendary science fiction writer Gene Roddenberry) is not only respected but admired by Captain Jean-Luc Picard. In the episode "The Measure of a Man" written by novelist Melinda M. Snodgrass, a scientist wants to dismantle Data to make replicas of him. His efforts are stymied when, following Picard's fiery objections in court, a Starfleet judge rules that Data is not property—not a mere machine to be used and discarded at will—but a valuable member of the crew.

Authors and screenwriters invent engaging and aspirational creatures that can complete tasks that are and will always be impossible for humans, such as speaking hundreds of languages and working without sleep. These writers introduce audiences to technical concepts well before anything like them appears in research labs. Their imaginations (and intelligence) engage our own, and, in turn, they're inspired by what is being invented by engineers, extrapolating possibilities from the roots of their discoveries. "From the very early days of science fiction, going all the way back to Jules Verne, there's been a feedback loop between real scientists and science fiction writers . . . we inspire each other," says Gary Whitta, a game designer, producer, and screenwriter who contributes to, among many other works, the Star Wars universe, where he had a hand in creating the droid K2SO for *Rogue One: A Star Wars Story*. Whitta also believes that science fiction plays a pivotal role in our fantasies of what artificial intelligence can and should deliver—not only in what we crave in today's marketplace, but also what we fear—and trust. "Hollywood has created unrealistic expectations for what AI is like, or can be like, or should be like."

Human-robot interaction is increasingly important in our real world; "agent theory" is a burgeoning area of AI research with applications in multiple fields. Yet, in 2022, we still have limited representation of truly functioning robots, beyond what are basically beta-level self-driving cars, digital assistants, industrial line workers, and vacuum cleaners. These pale in comparison to robots that could be our servants, fight beside us, or even be our friends.

Is AI behind, or are our hopes skewed? What should we expect from robots in the twenty-first century and beyond? As we'll discuss throughout the book, engineers, industrial designers, and programmers are discovering more and more ways that robots can contribute to society, including in the fields of agriculture, defense, health care, and transportation. Each day brings new announcements of AI breakthroughs and exciting applications, including the development of senses, including taste and touch (or haptic feedback), for these mechanical creatures. Such nuances will deliver more useful machines, and inch us closer to those anthropomorphized robots of science fiction. And while Hollywood's level of possibilities may never be fully realized, living, self-healing skin for robots is the focus of a University of Tokyo lab. As invention proceeds, perhaps Isaac Asimov's Three Laws of Robotics from his 1942 short story "Runaround" remain our best guidelines:

> **First Law:** A robot may not injure a human being or, through inaction, allow a human being to come to harm.

> **Second Law:** A robot must obey the orders given it by human beings except where such orders would conflict with the First Law.

> **Third Law:** A robot must protect its own existence as long as such protection does not conflict with the First or Second Law.

Whether you're an early adopter, buying each new AI device available, or fear the advent of smart machines that could replace human workers (or worse), through the spirit of entrepreneurial energy, the compounding intellect of researchers in the field, and the drive for efficiencies, robots will be a bigger and bigger part of our futures, regardless of if we're aware of all their roles.

FURTHER READING

Tony Ho Tran, "Experimental Rover Allows Astronauts to 'Feel' What the Robot Touches," *Daily Beast,* April 20, 2022, https://www.thedailybeast.com/experimental-european -space-agency-rover-allows-astronauts-to-feel-what-the-robot-touches.

Miriam Fauzia, "This Robot Chef Is Learning to Taste and Cook Food Like a Human," *Daily Beast,* May 4, 2022, updated May 9, 2022, https://www.thedailybeast.com/this-robot -chef-is-learning-to-taste-and-cook-food-like-a-human?ref=home.

Alison Snyder, "Scientists Create a Robotic Finger with Living Skin, *Axios,* June 13, 2022, https://www.axios.com/2022/06/13/robotic-finger-living-human-skin.

INTELLIGENT MACHINES

It took nearly a decade to design and build the first interactive "intelligent" computer program, although its capabilities might seem rudimentary to us now. Joseph Weizenbaum, a German-American computer scientist at MIT, built ELIZA, a program that could carry on a conversation (of sorts) with a human, between 1964 and 1966. Many people took it to be an electronic therapist, but ELIZA was more of a rudimentary chatbot: The user would type in a statement, press the enter key, and receive a response from the machine. Using pattern matching and substitution methodology, ELIZA (named for Eliza Doolittle, the cockney heroine of the Broadway musical *My Fair Lady* who learns to speak with an upper-class accent) gave canned responses that made users feel as if they were communicating with someone who understood their questions. In reality, ELIZA simply turned the questions back to the "patient." Weizenbaum explained that people would spend hours at the keyboard "talking" to ELIZA. Here's an example of a conversation between ELIZA and a "patient."

> *Human:* Men are all alike.
>
> *Computer:* IN WHAT WAY?
>
> *Human:* They're always bugging us about something or other.
>
> *Computer:* CAN YOU THINK OF A SPECIFIC EXAMPLE?

Human: Well, my boyfriend made me come here.
Computer: YOUR BOYFRIEND MADE YOU COME HERE?
Human: He says I'm depressed much of the time.
Computer: I AM SORRY TO HEAR YOU ARE DEPRESSED.
Human: It's true. I am unhappy.[19]

The success of ELIZA revealed that the *simulation* of artificial intelligence was enough to fool many people, including Weizenbaum's secretary, who asked that other people clear the room and give her privacy to talk to the machine, which was built with a mere 200 lines of code.[20] (By comparison, an average iPhone app has about 50,000 lines of code, while Google's entire internet services contain about two billion lines of code.) Weizenbaum wrote of his surprise at how people reacted to ELIZA: "People who knew very well that they were conversing with a machine soon forgot the fact, just as theatergoers, in the grip of suspended disbelief, soon forget that the action they're witnessing is not 'real.' They would often demand to be permitted to converse with the system in private, and would, after conversing with it for a time— insist, in spite of my explanations, that the machine really understood them."[21] This anthropomorphizing of computer intelligence continues today. How many of us have yelled at our car's navigation system or personal digital assistant for not giving an answer that we wanted to hear? As humans and robots increasingly work together, bridging the communication gap is one of the big hurdles in the study of human-computer interaction.

THE FRUSTRATIONS OF AI

From chatbot to robot, the quest for artificial intelligence continued in the academic world. In the 1960s, Charles Rosen and a team at the Stanford Research Institute built Shakey, a wobbly robot that combined animal locomotion, perception, and problem-solving.[22] It was followed a decade later by the Stanford Cart, which became the first computer-controlled vehicle when it navigated a chair-filled room in the Stanford Artificial Intelligence Laboratory and helped lay the foundation for self-driving cars.

While some researchers pursued the dream of autonomous robots that could move, grasp, and communicate, others worked on the problem of intelligent algorithms—and how to make them work more efficiently and independently. The 1970s were a time of limited government funding and a dearth of confidence in the field of artificial intelligence, the first of several so-called AI winters that began in 1969 after Marvin Minsky and Seymour Papert, co-directors of the MIT Artificial Intelligence Laboratory, published *Perceptrons*, a book that raised concerns about the ability of an artificial neuron (known as a neural network) to find solutions to AI problems. The book was highly influential and cast some doubts on the possibility that AI could understand human language. It also came at a time when the Pentagon was beginning to redirect federal AI funding from basic research into specific military-related projects.

Stanford researchers built the experimental tool MYCIN in 1976 and programmed it with 450 rules to diagnose blood infections in human patients.[23] It performed better than most resident doctors as well as some experts in the field. MYCIN, named for the -mycin suffixes of antibiotics, was never actually used in a hospital, but it achieved a 65 percent accuracy rating in diagnosing infections, according to a 1979 study by Victor Yu and colleagues published in the *Journal of the American Medical Association*,[24] as compared with a rating of 45 to 62 percent among Stanford Medical School faculty, raising the question of how often medical experts disagree about a diagnosis—and attesting, perhaps, to their resistance to computerized assessments. MYCIN was built before the era of personal computers—it was a stand-alone system that required a user to enter information by typing in responses to questions the computer posed then running its diagnosis algorithm on a large time-shared computer system. That's not the most efficient way of figuring out what's ailing a patient, and perhaps not the most comforting one, either.

In 1980, Digital Equipment Corporation (DEC) unveiled the first computer system that ordered new parts for itself. The idea was to have the computer itself, rather than a human technician, figure out what parts needed to be replaced (similar to printers telling you when they need a new ink cartridge). It was developed at Carnegie Mellon University and rolled out in several DEC operations across the United States. By 1986, the XCON system was saving the firm an estimated $40 million a year through improved efficiencies.

The AI industry mushroomed from revenues of a few million dollars to billions of dollars.[25] By the early 1990s, however, most commercial artificial intelligence companies had failed, while other major firms like Texas Instruments and Xerox abandoned the field, according to Russell and Norvig. The $400 million Japanese government effort to deliver a fifth-generation computer that began in 1981 ended quietly in 1992 without reaching its goal of building a machine to think with the equivalent of human intelligence.[26]

NEURAL NETWORKS

While these commercial efforts failed, academic labs started working on a method to solve problems in AI called a neural network, an approach that had been nearly abandoned 20 years earlier. Inspired by the human brain, a neural network is composed of a series of computer algorithms that mimics the way brain cells communicate with each other to solve problems. Neural networks rely on training data to learn and improve their accuracy over time.[27]

In the early 2000s, researchers took a computer chip known as a graphical processing unit (GPU), which was originally designed for video games and had become more powerful than standard computer chips, and did something quite interesting. By fusing a GPU with a neural network, a group led by Geoff Hinton at the University of Toronto was able to achieve astounding success correctly identifying images from a database, known as ImageNet, of 1.3 million pictures sourced from the internet. Using existing machine-learning techniques, the best algorithms could score 75 percent, meaning they could identify a picture of a cat or a banana or any other object three out of four times. By training its algorithm with a deep-learning neural network and the GPU, the Toronto team reported a success rate of 84 percent in 2012. By 2017, that figure had jumped to 98 percent. The birth of deep learning can be tied to this influential experiment and the 2012 paper by Hinton and graduate students Alex Krizhevsky and Ilya Sutskever, "ImageNet Classification with Deep Convolutional Neural Networks."[28]

Deep learning hinges on the algorithm making generalizations based on large amounts of data using trial and error rather than following a specific set of instructions. Deep-learning algorithms are hungry for big amounts of data so that they can train themselves. That's how DeepMind's algorithm AlphaGo was able to defeat human champions in the 2,500-year-old Chinese territory-acquisition game Go—by playing 30 million games to reach that capability level, something that a human player could never do in a lifetime. It's also how IBM's chess-playing computer Deep Blue defeated grandmaster Garry Kasparov in 1997.

SENSORS: KEY BUILDING BLOCKS OF AI

Advances in artificial intelligence occur in step with developments in their supporting technologies, such as sensors computing at macro and micro scales, communication networks, and data storage. The ability of algorithms to directly interface with data collected by microphones, cameras, medical imaging scanners, bio-signals, global positioning system sensors, and financial and medical records is enabling AI as a powerful force in commerce and society.

Since 2012, when the deep-learning tool AlexNet was developed at the University of Toronto, the sensor-to-reasoning pipeline has shown remarkable performance improvements in many computer vision tasks such as object and face detection and verification, as well as speech-recognition digital assistants. The floodgates have opened. To grasp where we are today, it's worth remembering where sensor technology was a half- century ago. In the 1960s and '70s, images and videos were captured by bulky, low-resolution still and television cameras that produced blurry images, especially when the person or the platform holding the cameras (or the objects themselves) was in motion. As semiconductor technologies advanced in the 1980s, new digital cameras were able to capture higher volumes of pixels that make up each image, giving them clearer resolution. The cameras also became smaller. Today we have high-resolution digital video cameras in cell phones, cars, drones, and other platforms. As processing of images improved with better semiconductor chips, so too did new camera designs known as omni-directional cameras, which enabled 360-degree views of a scene. Today these are installed in hotels, retail stores, and public spaces and on buildings, and they are part of what makes surveillance possible.

Traditional video cameras collect a sequence of two-dimensional frames. From the mid-1980s onwards, industrial applications needed the acquisition of three-dimensional images that added depth. In the 1980s these sensors, known as LADARs (for laser detection and ranging) were heavy and slow. Improved 3D sensors are available these days, many of them finding applications in self-driving cars and industrial inspection tasks. In the early 2000s Microsoft introduced a type of camera called Kinect that produced 3D data as well as video frames. Production of the cameras, used primarily in games and other indoor navigation and mapping applications, stopped in 2017, but in 2018, a new suite of Kinect 2 cameras was introduced for artificial intelligence applications. In the past decade, Kinect 2 cameras have been used in surgical suites to create 3D images of internal organs and to control robotic arms on NASA space vehicles.[29] Microsoft's Azure Kinect DK platform is now used for many applications that combine forms of virtual reality, 3D mapping, and AI.[30]

The automobile industry has adopted these advanced sensors along with object recognition in a big way to make their cars safer and more efficient. Some companies used video cameras and 3D sensors in their vehicles, while Tesla engineers decided to rely solely on video cameras to sense objects around the car. Self-driving cars have cameras and 3D depth sensors, and many of us already enjoy the benefits of increased automation and safety measures such as blind spot warning, smart cruise control, lane change warnings, and automatic braking.

While most cameras used in AI and computer vision operate in the visible part of the electromagnetic spectrum, night-vision cameras capture the heat signature of an individual or object using infrared light, which is not visible to the human eye. Originally driven by military applications, thermal infrared cameras are finding more use in wildlife conservation and commercial surveillance applications to monitor facilities and warehouses.

Global positioning system (GPS) sensors and inertial measurement units (IMUs), which were initially developed for military use, now enable AI-powered vehicles and robotic devices to know where they are in relation to the human operator or other objects.[31] Gone are the frustrating days of carrying folded maps and road atlases (although some miss the joy of finding new places of interest by simply getting lost). GPS sensors in cell phones, cameras, and cars allow us—and cars and robots independently—to navigate freely, while small and powerful microphones can pick up our voices from across a room and send those signals to voice-activated devices.

While the availability of sensors mentioned above has helped accelerate the development of AI, the story isn't that simple. AI algorithms also need annotations or a tag to understand and exploit the data. Imagine these as tiny sticky notes telling the algorithm what's on the image or file. Annotations include guidance on object, scene type, identity, and the gender of a face. They're not typically generated by sensors but by humans who manually attach the tags to each digital file, and work for operations such as Amazon's Mechanical Turk, a crowdsourcing website for businesses to hire remotely located workers to perform discrete on-demand tasks that computers are currently unable to do.

Enormous amounts of digital data are being generated each year (64 zetabytes in 2020, which is 64 billion one-terabyte hard drives, each of which contain 250 HD movies). In the next five years, the amount of digital data created will be twice the amount created since the beginning of digital storage.[32] This vast ocean of digital data fuels the rise of artificial intelligence algorithms which are hungry for information. Today, new kinds of artificial intelligence systems are being designed that will tap into this growing amount of data without needing to read annotations.

Known by various names (self-supervised, unsupervised), these new methods will enable the development of innovative AI devices that operate directly on the collected data and lead to widespread use of AI in internet-connected devices, household appliances, smart phones, cars, tablets, and other portable devices such as health-monitoring units.

DEEP-LEARNING SPINOFFS

More than two decades after its introduction by Yann LeCun, the field of deep learning has become a blockbuster technology that is deployed by hundreds of companies. NASA engineers used deep learning to plan and execute complex operations for its spacecraft, while a machine-learning program on the NASA Mars Reconnaissance Observer sorts through images to detect craters that may hold water, ice, and perhaps the remnants of extraterrestrial life.[33] Deep-learning algorithms combined with natural language processing pushed the field of comprehension and translation. In 2019, Alibaba's reading comprehension program narrowly beat humans in a test at Stanford.[34] "These kinds of tests are certainly useful benchmarks for how far along the AI journey we may be," Microsoft spokesperson

Andrew Pickup told CNN in 2018. "However, the real benefit of AI is when it is used in harmony with humans."[35]

During the past decade, the explosion of deep-learning advancements has boosted the ability to translate languages, understand language, and identify photographs. It has also led to concerns that nefarious agents could harness AI. In 2014, Canadian researcher Ian Goodfellow invented generative adversarial networks (GANs), a method by which an algorithm is able to create something of its own by training on past images or data.[36] But the same GAN also enables deepfakes—computer-generated images and videos that can be nearly impossible to distinguish from real ones, such as one of Ukraine's president, Volodymyr Zelensky, asking his soldiers to surrender to Russia that was removed by Facebook in March 2022.[37]

Today, artificial intelligence is part of the toolkit of modern computer science and everyday life. It's also a vital component of any company or business that relies on digital information about its inventory, logistics, client base, or workforce. At the same time, some social critics are finding that artificial intelligence systems can exhibit bias, and the discussion of how to compensate for it in training sets of data has become a dominant theme at conferences and in public discourse. This sentiment of responsible or ethical AI being developed in the academic world is expressed by Olga Russakovsky, assistant professor of computer science at Princeton University. Russakovsky says that people are just now fully comprehending the power of artificial intelligence and the responsibility to guide it ethically. "We saw all of these potential applications, but it just wasn't working. Now some of the things are starting to work, with facial recognition being one of them. And so, as we started deploying it, it has good applications, and it has bad applications. This raises a lot of questions about bias in the technology around concentration of power and the good- and bad-use cases of it."[38] Russakovsky says that public debate about bias is happening around facial recognition because it has advanced further than other fields of artificial intelligence. Facial recognition is being used to guide corporate recruiters' decisions about who to hire, whether a bank grants a mortgage, and whether police decide to arrest someone.

Artificial intelligence, built and guided by human intelligence, psychology, and emotions, has the capacity to amplify all of our best and worst qualities. In the next chapter we'll look at how AI has changed medical practice and how medical professionals, while driven by the possibilities, are grappling with both the technical limitations of AI and its social implications for patient care and individual privacy.

CHAPTER 2

Saving Lives with AI

THE USE OF ARTIFICIAL INTELLIGENCE in the field of medicine has exploded in the past few years, and AI is now being used in applications everywhere from research labs to surgical suites. Just as computer vision and facial recognition push the boundaries of both security and automated vehicles—topics I'll explore in the chapters that follow—they also are having huge impacts on medicine. I've collaborated with several researchers in the past few years to use the tools of computer vision, such as powerful cameras, to improve the accuracy of algorithms that can identify a medical condition by scanning an image.

I've been fascinated by how technology can and could help medicine and health care since my undergraduate student days in India. For our senior project in 1975, my partner and I designed a pacemaker using transistors. Because integrated circuits weren't available at the time for us to build a system that could be implanted in a human, the pacemaker looked more like a small radio with blinking LED lights. Of course, we never got to try it out in a patient, but at that time, biomedical signal and image processing was developing into an active research area—one that I was eager to join. During my graduate studies at Purdue University, I concentrated in the growing field of computer vision. I designed algorithms to allow a computer to see the world around it, which later led to object recognition and facial recognition. These are ways that an algorithm classifies the images it sees. But applications in medicine were on the horizon.

When I joined the faculty of the University of Southern California in 1981, a senior colleague, George Bekey, introduced me to analyzing electromyographic (EMG) signals, which help assess the health of tissue and muscles. We submitted a National Science Foundation (NSF) grant proposal and received a three-year grant to research how, given recordings of skin surface EMG signals, we could estimate the signals between muscles, rather than sticking a needle directly into the patient's muscle tissue to measure the signals. We developed several algorithms to reconstruct these signals, which were tested on signal data that were artificially generated. The results from the experiment were both encouraging and depressing. While I appreciated the great benefits of applying technology to medicine, I also understood the complexity of biomedical signal processing. I became more acutely aware of how extremely difficult it is to model something as complicated as the human body using mathematical equations.

While we weren't ultimately successful in this particular project, the quest to design and build such a sensor has continued with other researchers over the years. Today, non-invasive skin sensors for EMG signals are being used to monitor infants,[1] to determine fatigue levels for athletes, and to diagnose various kinds of muscular disorders. As with many medical devices, while the initial technological innovation can happen in a few years, getting that product through the clinical testing, patent application, and regulatory pipeline can take decades.

In 1985, I received a Presidential Young Investigator Award and decided to switch fields from signal processing to computer vision and pattern recognition. For a long time, I was focused on projects for DARPA. It was almost 2003 when I again ventured into medical applications of the technology. While at the University of Maryland, Stanford professor Thomas P. Andriacchi and I were awarded a five-year, $2.5 million grant from the National Science Foundation to develop markerless motion capture methods using computer vision methods. Motion capture technology has been used for decades for detecting and monitoring motion-related disorders, and has both diagnostic and rehabilitative uses. For many years, researchers had used small markers attached to limbs and joints to record the motion as patients walk on a treadmill or move a body part. The markers send a signal to a computer program that can be used to detect movement-related disorders, monitor patients' recovery from knee surgery and hip replacement, or diagnose gait disorders. Markerless motion capture systems, on the other hand, do the same thing without using the little tags. The advantages of a markerless system were patient comfort and convenience. The tags often fell off the patients' skin if not attached properly, and for elderly people with sensitive skin, the tags could be painful, which drove us to find an alternative.

From 2003 to 2008, Andriacchi and I collaborated on the development of several eight camera–based markerless motion capture systems. One of them was tested and validated on clinical patients, a rewarding result for our efforts to translate laboratory technology to human patients.[2] In the fifteen years since then, markerless motion capture has advanced and is now able to construct two-dimensional and three-dimensional images of human body poses.[3] In effect, this technology allows a computer to see the shape and movement of a human body, which is important for diagnosing neurological disorders like Parkinson's and Huntington's disease as well as improving the performance of athletes, including several major league baseball clubs, the LAFC soccer team, and professional golfers who use it to improve their swing.[4]

The combination of computer vision and medicine also has applications for treating heart conditions. In 2013, a couple of my University of Maryland computer engineering students and I teamed up with Mark Smith, a specialist in diagnostic radiology and nuclear medicine, and Timm-Michael Dickfeld, an electrophysiologist. Together we developed a new software tool to integrate electrical signals from the heart with data from two kinds of scanning technologies—positron emission tomography (PET) and single-photon emission computed tomography (SPECT). The tool helped surgeons get more information about the shape and condition of the heart muscle and perform certain operations more quickly and effectively.

I remember from the several meetings I had with the University of Maryland School of Medicine team that Dr. Dickfeld, after completing a six-hour procedure, would walk into our meetings in scrubs and get involved in detailed technical conversations about computer vision algorithms. I was impressed by his enthusiasm and open-mindedness—his willingness to incorporate new technologies into established practices with the goal of helping his patients.

Over the past eighteen months my group at Hopkins has developed new approaches to help surgeons detect and avoid metallic implants using sophisticated tools of medical image reconstruction. We've also developed algorithms for synthesizing novel views of X-rays that can assist physicians in interpreting anatomy more reliably. These programs are still being developed, so are not yet ready for commercial applications. We look forward to the day when they will help improve surgical capacities, and save patients' lives.

When an opportunity arose for me to explore the medical uses of machine learning and AI, I decided to embrace it wholeheartedly. I'm excited by the possibility of what can be achieved when the best minds from machine learning and AI work together with leading doctors and clinical researchers; Johns Hopkins is the perfect place to explore this. But while the rewards could be immeasurable, the challenges are many. Until recently, the traditional approach for developing computer-based algorithms for different fields has been to customize them for each application. With the advent of new tools based on deep learning and machine learning, a common set of tools is used to diagnose different kinds of diseases. For example, methods for diabetic retinopathy and lung cancer detection could be based on similar deep-learning networks. This has increased the pace of moving from discovery in the laboratory to use and validation in a clinical setting, to commercial applications. While this is to be celebrated, it also introduces challenges inherent in purely data-driven approaches because the methodology may exhibit bias or lack generalization across various datasets. Because most deep-learning methods are based on models trained on a large set of images from the internet, developers must be careful not to assume that the same algorithm will work on very different-looking images of the human body, such as those detailing tissue, bone growth, or tumors.

In the next few pages, we'll explore what AI is already doing and where it could go to improve diagnosis, clinical care, and recovery. It's not often that we can witness the confluence of two good things coming together to make a great thing; this burgeoning field offers a great deal of promise for both patients and practitioners.

PREDICTING MORTALITY WITH AI

What if a computer program could predict when you'll die? At Stanford Hospital in Palo Alto, California, medical researchers have come up with a formula that does just that—which may sound morbid and alarming, but it has a compassionate use. The algorithm examines written orders that are documented in a patient's electronic health record to come up with a risk of mortality in the next three to 12 months. The researchers trained a deep-learning algorithm on two million records of patients admitted to the hospital. Any patient at a 75 percent or higher risk of dying is flagged. This number, however, isn't shared with the patient or even the attending physician. Instead, a red flag email arrives in the physician's inbox, prompting the doctor to begin discussing an uncomfortable subject: how to prepare for the possibility of death within the following year. "It's not really meant to tell the clinician how likely it is that the patient will die—it's a surrogate for highlighting which patients should have an advance care planning conversation," says Ron Li, a physician and medical informatics director for Digital Health and AI Clinical Integration at Stanford Medicine.[5]

Li and his team developed the program after realizing that doctors and other health care workers weren't talking about end-of-life care with their patients. Not only is it a difficult subject to bring up, but doctors' time with patients has been limited by an increased patient load, by keeping up with electronic record keeping, and by insurance company directives. "In a busy environment, it's hard to find a structured time to do it and document it," Li says about the end-of-life talk. "The way we designed this is that it integrates with their electronic health records—all you have to do is double-click the flag, and it allows you to reduce the friction of doing it." It becomes a documented step in the process, prompted at an appropriate time, rather than leaving the timing of the conversation up to the doctor's judgment and often hurried schedule.

One side benefit of the Stanford Hospital mortality prediction model is that nonphysicians on the staff are now feeling empowered to talk to patients about their wishes during the last few months of their life. In the past, that kind of intimate conversation with a terminal patient was the exclusive domain of the white coat–wearing doctor. Pooja Rao is an occupational therapist at Stanford Health Care who helps patients make their lives easier once they've recovered from illness and return home from the hospital. That could mean rearranging furniture, making the shower easier to access, or understanding movement patterns from the patient's bed to the bathroom in order to reduce falls. Rao says that the mortality risk program has become a valuable tool to talk patients through what's important in the final months of life without scaring them. "We definitely don't go into the room and say, 'Hey, you were identified on this algorithm, and we want to have this conversation with you,'" Rao says.[6] "It's more like, 'I'd like to talk to you about what understanding you have of your illness and what's important.'"

Rao remembers an older male patient with a host of underlying complications who came into the hospital with leg cellulitis, a condition that left him bedridden and at risk for further complications. "His leg was really red and swollen. He was barely able to walk," Rao says. "Before he came to the hospital, he was able to walk around independently, but then—once he came to the hospital—he was barely able to get up out of bed or get himself to the bathroom." After having a conversation with the patient upon receiving a red flag notification. Rao says the patient was willing to get an amputation if it was going to improve his quality of life.

Using the psychological opening that the AI mortality model provided, Rao learned what was most important to the patient and passed it on to his medical team. This kind of partnership between AI and human caregivers is becoming more common at other medical centers as well. Doctors in the University of Pennsylvania Health System quadrupled the number of advance care conversations after using the machine-learning algorithm in their clinical practice, according to a study of 15,000 patients published in 2020 in the journal *JAMA Oncology*.[7] The algorithm considers more than 500 variables—age, number of hospitalizations, and comorbidities, for example—from patient records through their most recent appointment.

The program also boosted the number of end-of-life conversations between doctors and ethnic or minority groups by dispelling myths that physicians might have about how members of these groups discuss death. "It's actually putting data in front of clinicians as opposed to letting them rely on potential biases," says Ravi Parikh, assistant professor of medical ethics and policy and medicine at the University of Pennsylvania. "You get a text message that counters the natural presumptions you might have," he says.[8]

The advanced care discussion algorithm doesn't do as well with leukemia or bone marrow transplant patients, nor is it ready to predict rates of hospitalization or disease progression, according to Parikh. It's another tool for physicians and health care workers—a very powerful one—but not a crystal ball. "We don't want a machine making decisions," Parikh says, "whether it's something benign, like having a conversation, or more intensive, like whether someone should get a liver transplant. I think that when we rely on algorithms or machines to do that solely for us, we're losing a human element—how we practice medicine. In this case, what the algorithm does is largely make sense of a lot of complicated and disparate sources of information that the clinician doesn't always have time to read and process."

Some of the biggest AI-related changes in health care are happening in imaging. In May 2019, Google unveiled a system that it said outperformed six radiologists in determining whether patients had lung cancer, which causes more deaths (180,000) in the United States than any other cancer.[9] The system detected 5 percent more cancers and cut false positives by 11 percent. About 75 percent of lung cancer patients die within five years of diagnosis, but only 16 percent of patients are diagnosed within the first year, when a successful treatment is more likely. When the tumors are found early—when they're smaller and confined to the lungs—almost two thirds of patients survive for at least five years. FDA officials approved more than 160 AI-driven products over the past six years, with the vast majority focused on analyzing data coming from CT scanners, MRI machines, and other imaging devices.[10]

In July 2020, the University of Oxford in England announced a $14.3 million research program to use AI to help diagnose lung cancer by combining clinical, imaging, and molecular data while also reducing invasive clinical procedures. The addition of biomarkers for genetic data is a big step forward. The Oxford program will also develop algorithms to better evaluate risks from comorbidities such as chronic obstructive pulmonary disease (COPD). These developments intend to make lung-cancer screening more precise and accessible, but they'll also require a close relationship between radiologists and the machines.

PREDICTING PATIENT OUTCOMES

Jeffrey Siewerdsen, a professor of biomedical engineering at Johns Hopkins University, has developed a machine-learning algorithm to detect the best candidates for spinal surgery based on X-ray and MRI images. Previously, surgeons assessed surgical candidates based on their age, body mass index, gender, comorbidities including risk factors such as diabetes, and whether they smoked. Siewerdsen wanted to know if he could predict patients' health trajectories after surgery as well, and whether they also needed aggressive physical therapy or rehabilitation. "We were extracting features of the patient's spinal morphology from the imaging data," Siewerdsen says, "and what we found is that not only were predictive models more accurate when we could image, but they were driving the model. Nine out of ten of the most important features were from the image."[11]

Siewerdsen and the surgeons with whom he collaborates assumed that a patient's overall health would be the biggest influence on how well they recover from surgery, but the machine-learning algorithm found that the shape of the patient's spine was actually the more critical indicator of recovery. It has allowed Siewerdsen and the surgeons involved to make better decisions about what kind of spinal interventions to use—where to place screws or remove tissue, for example—and to give their patients a better understanding of how they'll do after surgery—or whether surgery is indeed the best option. Siewerdsen built his model over two years and tested it on 200 cases. As with many AI-in-medicine algorithms, its accuracy is based on the demographics of the patients. The clinic that Siewerdsen used for his study sees some of the most advanced cases of spinal surgery; other clinics in other cities might have a different patient population with less severe cases or patients who are younger or in better physical condition, for example.

Shifting the Hopkins predictive spine surgery model to another hospital would require that it be retrained with a new patient population, he explains. That's relatively simple from a statistical standpoint, but less clear is how that so-called shift in data would need to be approved by health care regulators in each state or by the federal government. Currently, when a new drug or medical device is approved, everyone has access to it. But with a new AI algorithm that may increase the odds of survival or a better outcome after surgery, it depends to some extent on who your doctor is at the hospital. For AI to grow in acceptance by both patients and the public, at least in the field of medicine, that informed oversight is vital.

For data scientists, the health care industry is an extraordinary resource. Hospitals and health care workers collect loads of data from patients each day in the form of high-resolution images, vital signs details, doctors' orders, diagnostic exams, and genetic tests. Genomic data alone are predicted to be in the range of 2–40 exabytes by 2025—eclipsing the amount of data acquired by YouTube, Twitter, and the entire field of astronomy.[12] This boom in medical data has become possible because of increased computational power and the growing use of off-site cloud storage rather than computer servers hosted at each hospital or medical facility.

As detailed in the aforementioned cases, image recognition and machine-learning algorithms can sift through this patient data to find unexpected patterns and connections that might elude humans—even teams of humans—with decades of combined training and experience. When used together with the expertise of a doctor or radiologist, AI can improve decision-making, reduce errors in both diagnoses and procedures, and streamline a patient's experience through what can be a confusing and often dehumanizing experience—a trip to the hospital. Algorithms designed by teams of doctors and machine-learning experts are identifying tumors and tissue growths faster than human radiologists working alone; they're also detecting early signs of eye disease, melanomas, cardiac abnormalities, and childhood genetic disorders through use of facial recognition.

These number-crunching programs are also helping hospital managers better understand one of the trickiest decisions about a sick person: whether the patient should remain in the hospital or return home to recuperate. With the average cost of a three-day hospital stay at $30,000 and the overall cost of health care in the United States blowing past the $4 trillion mark in 2020,[13] figuring out how best to manage patient care promises to lower costs for everyone.

Administrators, insurance companies, and medical practice managers are using the tools of AI to help improve efficiencies in their local hospital or regional health group. One of the promises of these algorithms is that by marrying computing power and statistical strength, AI can come up with the optimal solution for a hospital's workflow and billing practices, given the right amount, size, and kind of information. The paradox of AI and health care is that even as these digital technologies are thirsty for big data, electronic health records are often stuck into smaller digital boxes that can't be combined with other data. Unlike national systems in Canada, the United Kingdom, or Europe, health care in the United States is segmented into separate groups backed by private insurance plans or the federal Medicare/Medicaid system. Privacy laws also limit data sharing, even when the patient's name is removed from the information, especially for rare conditions or diseases. That makes assembling big national or multistate databases about health care for optimal AI system references more difficult in the United States than in other countries.

At the same time, a 2020 study published in *JAMA* found

that health care researchers who are building predictive AI algorithms for some conditions only use patients who live nearby or in urban areas near large medical centers, which limits the ability to validate how well these programs work.[14] Having a large national database of health records would make this task easier.

The *JAMA* authors reviewed 71 studies from 2015 to 2019 that used deep-learning algorithms to perform an image-based diagnostic task in radiology, ophthalmology, dermatology, pathology, gastroenterology, and cardiology. They found that 56 of them used data from patients in California, Massachusetts, or New York. Among the remaining 47 states, 34 did not contribute any patient data. That means that almost all these AI health care algorithms are being trained on folks living in large urban areas while vast swaths of the country's population are being overlooked. Does that mean the algorithms aren't accurate? Not necessarily, but it does mean that whoever is using them must be aware of their limitations and adjust accordingly. Rural and suburban populations differ by smoking and obesity rates, for example, as well as their access to health care. That needs to be factored into any algorithms used by health centers that serve a rural population. At the same time, some observers worry the hype over AI may blind doctors, administrators, and researchers to some of the limitations of these technological tools in predicting the course of a disease or efficacy of a specific treatment. Other critics are raising concerns over potential bias against minorities embedded in an algorithm's code. One 2019 study in the journal *Science* found that analytics software often reinforces inequalities in the US health care system.[15] The report found that the bias occurred because the algorithm predicted health care costs rather than illnesses, even though unequal access to care has led to less money spent caring for Black patients than for white patients. While health care costs appear to be an effective measure for health by some forms of predictive accuracy, it also led to racial biases, according to authors Ziad Obermeyer, Brian Powers, Christine Vogeli, and Sendhil Mullainathan.

Another study found that AI tools could worsen disparities in the detection and treatment of breast cancer, a disease that is 46 percent more likely to be fatal for Black women. "The bias is not intentional, but it reinforces deeply rooted inequities in the American health care system, effectively walling off low-income Black and Hispanic patients from services that less sick white patients routinely receive," according to a 2020 article by the Boston-based health news platform *STAT*.[16]

How does racial and gender bias happen when AI is deployed in health care? Sometimes, it's a matter of the researcher not considering how narrowly representative the demographic or ethnic group being sampled is. First, *statistical* bias is common in predictive algorithms for many reasons, including less than optimal sampling, measurement error in predictor variables, and heterogeneity of effects. For example, the Framingham Study is a well-known long-term longitudinal study of more than 5,200 residents of the town of Framingham, Massachusetts, that began in 1948.[17] Medical researchers carefully followed these people over three generations, measuring their diet, weight, and risk factors such as smoking. In more recent years, the study has expanded to include sampling of genetic information. Because of the large size of the study, it has become a medical treasure trove for understanding the prevalence and associated risk of various conditions from heart disease to dementia. Dozens of important epidemiological studies have been completed since the Framingham Study began, but there's one problem: The original group was overwhelmingly white, and so when medical researchers apply the Framingham Risk Score for heart disease to populations with similar clinical characteristics, the predicted risk of a cardiovascular event was 20 percent lower for Black individuals compared with white individuals. That means that the score may not adequately capture an accurate health risk for some minority groups that weren't sampled in the original Framingham Study.[18]

A 2020 study of Black and white kidney patients in the Boston area documented how a widely used algorithm for estimating kidney function that by design assigns Black people healthier scores, ended up making it tougher for them to qualify for a transplant. The study published in the *Journal of the*

Annals of Internal Medicine analyzed health records for 57,000 people with chronic kidney disease from the Mass General Brigham health system, which includes Harvard teaching hospitals Massachusetts General and Brigham and Women's.[19] One-third of 2,225 Black patients—more than 700 people— would have been placed into a more severe category of kidney disease if their kidney function had been estimated using the same formula as for white patients. That could have affected decisions such as when to refer someone to a kidney specialist or for a kidney transplant. In 64 cases, the study found, patients' recalculated scores would have qualified them for placement on a kidney-transplant waiting list. None had been referred or evaluated for transplant, suggesting that doctors didn't question the race-based recommendations.

Social bias also compounds the racial bias of some health care algorithms. Artificial intelligence is likely to incorrectly estimate risks for patients with missing data in their electronic health record. For example, among women with breast cancer, Black women had a lower likelihood than white women of being tested for high-risk germline mutations, despite both groups having a similar risk of such mutations. Thus, an AI algorithm that depends on genetic test results is more likely to mischaracterize the risk of breast cancer for Black patients than for white patients. One of the concerns, as pointed out by the authors of a report on AI-related bias in health care published in *JAMA* in 2019, is that doctors look for information that supports their preconceptions. "Perhaps of more concern," the authors wrote, "clinicians may be more likely to believe AI that reinforces current practice, thus perpetuating implicit social biases." Psychologists call the idea that we seek out information that supports what we already believe *confirmation* bias. In medicine or science, that's not only foolhardy—it can be dangerous.

There's an old saw from computer science: garbage in, garbage out. If algorithms in health care are programmed with data from a biased process, then the output may be similarly biased. This is a significant challenge when using clinical data sources like electronic health records, insurance claims, or device readings because most of these data are generated as a consequence of fallible human decisions; for instance, blood pressure readings are often inaccurate, partly because of differing levels of staff training. An algorithm is only as good as the data it feeds on. Of course, there are ways to account for and correct bias. The simplest way is to sample a number of people belonging to minority groups in the data used to train an AI algorithm. Another solution, the authors of the 2019 *JAMA* study note, is to use unbiased data sources that don't depend on human judgment, such as information from noninvasive patient monitoring during a hospital stay, vital signs during surgery, or from the first hour a patient arrives in the emergency room. These datasets can be compiled and analyzed by AI algorithms before physicians pass on a clinical assessment.

COVID-19 AND AI

In early 2020, BlueDot, a Canadian firm, applied artificial intelligence methodologies to help epidemiologists track the first cases of the COVID-19 outbreak through airline ticketing data, animal and plant disease networks, and foreign-language news reports.[20] AI also assisted molecular biologists in uncovering the deadly virus's molecular structure, a key step in finding a way to thwart it. Public health officials in South Korea used facial recognition to identify so-called super-spreaders, allowing them to quickly track down those who may have been infected and thereby slowing the initial spread of the novel virus.[21]

When the COVID-19 pandemic hit the United States in the first few months of 2020, Brian Garibaldi, a Johns Hopkins associate professor of clinical medicine, met with his team of data researchers to see if they could figure out how to turn patient data into a predictive tool for physicians. Professor Garibaldi didn't consider himself a data person, but he understood the power of using algorithms to solve problems in clinical practice, such as tackling the pandemic that was infecting and overwhelming health care workers throughout the United States. Over the next two months in 2020, he and his team came up with an algorithm called the Severe COVID-19 Adaptive Risk Predictor (SCARP). They wanted to help doctors get an idea of how COVID-19 patients would fare after being admitted to the hospital for a one- or two-week stay. The model relied on demographic characteristics, admission source, preexisting conditions, vital signs, laboratory measurements, and clinical severity during the patient's hospitalization.

Garibaldi and his team trained SCARP on more than three thousand COVID-19 patients at five hospitals in Washington, DC, and Maryland over several months as the outbreak expanded. The biggest challenge was adjusting data from various electronic health records so that the model could compare information compiled in different formats. Still, SCARP accurately predicted whether a patient would develop a severe case of illness over the next 24 hours with 89 percent accuracy, and a seven-day prediction with 83 percent accuracy, according to a study of the SCARP results published in the *Annals of Internal Medicine*.[22] The algorithm gave doctors in COVID-19 wards the ability to triage which patients needed more attention on a daily basis. "There are certain patients where you can walk into the room, you can speak with them, you can examine them, and you have a pretty good sense that this is someone who's at very high risk, and that can lead you to order certain therapies," Garibaldi says. "But we're not always able to predict seven days in advance."

Garibaldi's algorithm worked well enough to give doctors an early warning for choosing treatment and managing the flow of patients at the hospital. "We were making decisions about which new COVID-19 units to open, how many transfers from outside hospitals we could accept when other regions were overwhelmed, and whether or not we needed to think about scaling back elective surgical procedures to open up additional ICU beds," Garibaldi says. That kind of patient management might not have been possible without SCARP. Despite the team's success, most efforts by researchers to unleash the data-sniffing tools of AI algorithms on the COVID-19 pandemic didn't work as well: Only a handful made a difference at either detecting the virus from a chest scan or predicting the patient's risk of severe health problems or death, according to a review of 227 COVID-19 algorithms published in 2021 in the *British Medical Journal* (*BMJ*): "The majority of studies developed new models specifically for Covid-19, but only 46 carried out an external validation, and calibration was rarely assessed. We cannot yet recommend any of the identified prediction models for widespread use in clinical practice, although a few diagnostic and prognostic models originated from studies that were clearly of better quality. We suggest that these models should be further validated in other datasets, and ideally by independent investigators."[23] The *BMJ* study found that doctors and software engineers who created these COVID-19 prediction algorithms (used in the United States, Europe, and China) often didn't check their results, made assumptions about their patient populations that were incorrect, and ultimately didn't help their patients.

This assessment was reinforced by another large review carried out by researchers at the University of Cambridge and published in 2021 in the journal *Nature Machine Intelligence* (*NMI*).[24] This team analyzed deep-learning models for diagnosing COVID-19 and predicting patient risk from medical images, such as chest X-rays and chest computer tomography (CT) scans. They reviewed 415 published tools and, like the *BMJ* study, concluded that none were fit for clinical use. Neither the *BMJ* or *NMI* studies reviewed the SCARP model. "This pandemic was a big test for AI and medicine," Derek Driggs, a machine-learning researcher at the University of Cambridge and an author of the study told *MIT Technology Review* in 2021.[25] "It would have gone a long way to getting the public on our side. But I don't think we passed that test."

It's important to remember that information about COVID patients, including medical scans, was collected and shared in the middle of a global pandemic, often by the same doctors who were struggling to treat those patients. That meant that many of these machine-learning algorithms were built using mislabeled data or data from unknown sources or spliced together from multiple sources. Some tools ended up being tested on the same data they were trained on, making them appear more accurate than they were. During the first surge of the pandemic in 2020, hospitals and health care workers were buckling under the strain of a novel virus that they couldn't diagnose or treat. Just as ineffective cures were promoted (does anyone remember hydroxychloroquine?), so too did doctors rely on algorithms that weren't checked on big enough datasets. Experts say it takes time and lots of data points to validate algorithms, two factors that have been in short supply during this pandemic. But as medical researchers gain a deeper understanding of how the virus affects patients with various preexisting conditions and demographic backgrounds, it's likely they will fine-tune their algorithms and boost their accuracy. Garibaldi says the SCARP algorithm needs constant tweaks to maintain its accuracy, such as training it on clinical data from the Delta variant of COVID-19, which emerged in mid-2021.

Garibaldi hopes that a clinical trial based on a larger population of patients might help determine which kind of treatment or intervention could make a difference at an earlier stage of the disease. "What we don't know as well is if I give them dexamethasone a day early or oxygen earlier, would that make them better faster and get them out of the hospital?" Garibaldi asks. "That's really the Holy Grail right now."

In late 2021, AI-based algorithms were also deployed to fight the emerging Omicron variant. One scientist, computational genomics researcher Colby Ford at the University of North Carolina at Charlotte, developed a software program to predict how well existing vaccines might work against the Omicron variant using amino acids encoded in its genome. It took Ford about an hour to get his results and then publish them online. He was able to accurately predict that the new variant would be of concern and that some antibodies to previous COVID-19 strains would be less effective against Omicron several weeks before that was confirmed by laboratory studies.[26]

PREDICTING SEPSIS

The ability to carry an AI-powered prediction or clinical solution from the laboratory to the real world, where it can help people, is one of the challenges for AI-in-medicine researchers. Just ask Suchi Saria, professor of computer science at Johns Hopkins. Saria is a software and machine-learning expert who worked to develop health care data solutions for two decades as a graduate student at Stanford and as a professor at Hopkins since 2015. In 2016, while in her Baltimore apartment, Saria got a call from her family in India. Her normally healthy 26-year-old nephew had contracted a sepsis infection and was gravely ill. Coincidentally, at the time Saria had been working on the problem of using various bits of patient data for early detection of a possible sepsis infection in a hospital setting. In the United States, 750,000 patients develop severe sepsis and go into septic shock each year. More than half of them are admitted to an intensive care unit, accounting for 10 percent of all ICU admissions. They account for 20 to 30 percent of hospital deaths and $15.4 billion in annual health care costs.[27] But after her nephew died, she realized that she had a responsibility to move her solutions out of the laptop and lab and into the world. "I was sitting there, and it just sort of hit me that I had done all this work, but none of my work was having any real practical impact," Saria says. "I had gotten buried in this research world to a point where I had forgotten it needed to have practical applications for people."

Saria says that her focus expanded. Not only was it important to test and validate the sepsis-detection algorithm (which she and her colleagues did in 2015 and in 2021),[28] but it would also have to be something that a hospital or clinic could use on a regular basis. In addition, it was important for the program to be easy to operate while also functioning with a hospital's electronic medical-record system. "I thought the possibilities were now everywhere," Saria says. "The question was, what is it going to take to deliver value?" More questions followed. "How do you create inferences that are safe and trustworthy? How do you evaluate that it's working in the real world, not just in the lab?"

In 2018, Saria founded Bayesian Health (named for the eighteenth-century pioneer of probabilistic statistics, Thomas Bayes), a sepsis-prediction model startup. In July 2021, Bayesian emerged publicly with $15 million in venture capital funding with an AI tool that had spent more than three years in development and uses patents, peer-reviewed research, and technology licensed from the university.[29] Saria says that Bayesian's AI technology integrates every piece of available data from medical records, laboratory tests, and vital signs to equip doctors and nurses with accurate clinical signals that enable them to deliver the right care at the right time to save lives. Saria likens the artificial intelligence programs used by health care providers to the electronic signals robots use to move their arms. By late 2021, more than four thousand providers were using the Bayesian Health System.

Saria and her colleagues are now using the system to predict pressure ulcers (bed sores) and the sudden deterioration of a patient. She sees a future in which doctors, nurses, and other health care workers get real-time information about how to adjust both individual treatment plans and hospital workflow. The tools of artificial intelligence, large datasets, and powerful mobile computing are making this happen.

In a 2021 letter to the *New England Journal of Medicine*, Saria and seven colleagues pointed out various situations in which machine-learning methods developed using one set of data may not generalize to data collected for different hospital or patient populations.[30] A similar challenge arises when machine-learning methods are developed for analyzing pathology images prepared in different labs; the differences in staining processes often lead to what's known as a data-shift issue. Data shifts occur when the microscopes, medical scans or video cameras used by medical teams have slight differences in their resolution or image quality. These small differences between equipment in one lab and another can affect how the machine-learning algorithm identifies these images. That in turn can reduce the accuracy of the algorithm and possibly lead to a misdiagnosis. One solution my colleagues and I at Johns Hopkins are exploring is to train the algorithms to compensate for these differences.

Despite some limitations of AI, its use by doctors, hospitals, and health care providers will only continue to expand. From medical imaging to patient care, the tools of artificial intelligence are now firmly embedded in the nation's health care industry. Entrepreneurs and big tech firms like Amazon, Apple, Google, IBM, Microsoft, and NVIDIA are developing a separate but fast-growing AI-in-medicine industry of commercial applications that reached revenues of $6.7 billion in 2020, which is expected to expand at a compound annual growth rate of 41.8% from 2021 to 2028.[31]

Since the reemergence of deep learning–based algorithms, AI has moved from domain-based to data-driven mode. How-ever, for AI to be successful, domain knowledge that trained doctors have should be combined with data-driven AI. In medicine, there is no single domain knowledge, as the different diseases involve different kinds of domain knowledge or expertise and often need different kinds of data or measurements. Thus, we may have to develop quite a number of AI-based diagnosis and prediction methods to account for the numerous diseases that we need to take care of.

At the same time there have been a few flame-outs, like the January 2022 sale of IBM's Watson Health data and analytics business after a $4 billion investment by the tech firm failed to materialize. In 2020, the company dropped two AI-based cancer diagnosis products: Watson for Genomics and Watson for Oncology.[32] As artificial intelligence grows in the field of medicine, it will naturally face some bumps in terms of accuracy, unrealistic expectations, and bias—the same issues that AI faces in other sectors. Science is a field of trial and error. Not every experiment, not every enterprise, will succeed. But even the failures inform, and sometimes new, and successful, solutions are built from their rubble.

CHAPTER 3

The Complexities and Contributions of Facial Recognition

FACIAL RECOGNITION IS THE APPLICATION of artificial intelligence that tends to sound the loudest alarms. As with almost any technology, the impact of this series of digital tools depends on the human decisions informing their programming and guiding their use in myriad environments, under differing circumstances, and affecting a variety of communities. Half of US adults have their images stored in police face recognition databases, according to a 2016 report by Georgetown University's Center on Privacy and Technology.[1] Use of a facial ID scanner to screen people entering a secure building may not prompt much concern, but many consider deploying similar technology along a public street or in a park as intrusive, perhaps even authoritarian. Advocacy groups such as the American Civil Liberties Union say that its use by law enforcement agencies is an invasion of an individual's privacy, and they point to the technology's biases against certain groups.[2] Others note that, used properly, face recognition can speed identification of criminals; keep buildings, property, and airplanes safer; and aid in the rescue of missing and exploited children. In this chapter, we'll take a look at how the field of facial recognition and verification technology developed, how it works currently, where it needs adjustment, and what applications lie ahead.

My interest and work in facial recognition date back to the early 1990s, but computer vision and pattern recognition researchers and engineers have been developing the technology since the early 1970s. It's one of many biometric measurements that experts use to identify people including fingerprints, iris scans, speech recognition, and gait. Today, facial recognition is a software system that combines powerful digital cameras with deep-learning algorithms (computer programs that learn to process large amounts of data as the human brain would) that can match features from a person's face to an existing database of images. As face recognition technologies improved, the quality of facial images also improved thanks to the advances made in high-resolution camera designs. The evolution from the bulky television cameras of the 1960s and 1970s to present-day SLRs and handheld smartphone cameras has contributed to the success of face recognition algorithms. These cameras capture still images and video sequences, and compare them against an existing database of faces, such as state drivers' licenses or passport photos.

My colleagues and I have spent the past three decades making these systems more accurate and efficient. We've done so by accounting for variations in images of faces due to illumination, aging, and camera angles, as well as atmospheric distortions that come from images at a distance. We've also found ways to use computational power to make processing faster and to deter "deepfake" attacks that try to trick algorithms into using false facial images. Cameras and algorithms work better when faces and scenes are well lit, but less ideal conditions can be addressed by training the system on a larger set of faces so that it can recognize varied skin tones under different conditions. The matching accuracy of facial recognition algorithms today can exceed 95 percent—for certain categories of faces. In recent years, however, tests have shown that percentage to be lower for individuals with darker skin tones.

A 2018 study by the Massachusetts Institute of Technology found that some of the commercial applications for facial recognition, when applied for gender classification, demonstrated gender and skin-tone biases. The findings attracted widespread media attention and have had profound implications for the entire field of artificial intelligence. Many now believe that all forms of AI could be biased, but in fact the bias has been extensively studied in this one application of deep learning. I will consider the implications of the technology's bias later in this chapter.

Artificial intelligence is extremely powerful when matched to faces drawn from a large collection of images, including the billions of unique head shots taken over decades for driver's licenses, passports, and other forms of identification. However, a study performed from 2015 to 2017 with my colleagues at the University of Maryland Center for Automation Research, Alice O'Toole's group at the University of Texas, Dallas, and Jonathon Phillips's group at the National Institute of Standards and Technology found that while an AI-based algorithm performed better than human experts at recognizing faces, the most accurate results came when humans and computers worked together. The study, published in 2018 in the *Proceedings of the National Academy of Sciences*, compared the accuracy rates of several groups of people in identifying faces: professional forensic examiners; so-called super-recognizers who aren't professionally trained, but happen to have extraordinary skills; and a control group of college students.[4] The accuracy ranged from 68 percent for the students to 93 percent for the examiners. The study also compared several different facial recognition algorithms. Just as with humans, the accuracy varied among each one, from 68 percent to 96 percent.

THE BIRTH OF FACIAL RECOGNITION

Stanford graduate student Michael David Kelly's 1970 doctoral thesis, "Visual Identification of People by Computer," described an approach for human identification using face- and body-based measurements.[5] As with all early computer technology, his application used punch cards to input information into a computer in order to perform its calculations. In 1973, Takeo Kanade, a distinguished AI researcher at Carnegie Mellon University, developed an approach in his dissertation at Kyoto University that used the distances between key features for facial recognition.[6] In these early applications, the geometry of the face was mapped and then recorded by the computer.

Many facial recognition algorithms were developed over the next two decades, but they were tested only on small image datasets. The momentum for the next generation of face recognition systems came in 1991 in a landmark work from MIT by Matthew Turk, a graduate student, and Alex Pentland, a professor of computer science, who developed a method to translate an image of a human face into a series of numbers that can be understood by a computer.

Motivated by this work, in 1997 Peter Belhumeur of Columbia University, David Kriegman of the University of California, San Diego, and our group at the University of Maryland went a step further to develop a statistical representation that emphasized the slight differences between the faces of each subject. Christoph von der Malsburg's group at the University of Southern California developed another method in 1994 that placed a grid on the image of the human face in order to extract certain features that could be recognized by the computer. The US Army judged these three facial recognition algorithms as the most accurate in a 1997 evaluation. The military continued to use facial recognition, as well as fingerprints and iris scans, over the following decades, including during the war in Afghanistan beginning in 2016 as a way to verify the identity of local employees and reduce paycheck fraud. The system grew to include information about individuals working for US and coalition forces in Afghanistan. Unfortunately, in 2021 it was reported that the Taliban captured these biometric devices and their data, leading to fears that they would be used to target citizens who worked with the United States.[7]

Between 1996 and 2012, several approaches for facial recognition were developed using standard two-dimensional images, videos, and three-dimensional data. High-resolution video cameras captured depth and resulted in greater accuracy. Some of these algorithms were based on the geometry of the face, while others used features such as gender, hair color, ethnicity, eye color, and skin tone to match the image to an existing database.

There were sporadic attempts to deploy facial recognition technology for policing purposes at popular gathering places, such as the 2001 Super Bowl in Tampa, Florida, with the goal of identifying people who had jumped bail or committed other minor crimes. That was one of the first large-scale uses of facial recognition in the United States. Even though the system spotted 19 people thought to be subjects of outstanding warrants for minor crimes, none were arrested because the crowd was so large and the number of facial matches exceeded the expectations of the Tampa Police Department. "We thought we were ready to use it, but getting through the crowd and the architecture of the stadium proved overwhelming," Tampa police detective Bill Todd told the *New York Times* in July 2001.[8] Again, trial and error, and back to the drawing board.

Over the years, my group at the University of Maryland, and now at Johns Hopkins, has developed numerous approaches for facial recognition using 3D models of faces, video sequences, and face templates. With the support of the Office of Naval Research from 2008 to 2013, I led a team of researchers from Columbia University, the University of California, San Diego, and the University of Colorado, Colorado Springs, for building systems that would recognize faces at distances beyond 50 yards in maritime environments. We set up one experiment in Baltimore's Inner Harbor, putting volunteer subjects on one boat and the cameras on another. We took images of the subjects' faces when both boats were in motion and also from the shore when the passenger boat was moving in the harbor. We used commercially available sports photography–grade equipment for this experiment, but as part of the broader program, Professor Shree Nayar also built customized cameras for acquiring face images at distances beyond 150 yards.

We even simulated the scenario of face collection from an overhead drone aircraft by taking images from the top

Facial Recognition vs. the Master of Disguise

My years of research and development of facial recognition technologies and techniques have brought unexpected, and even fun, experiences to my labs. In early 2003, the staff of *National Geographic* magazine was preparing an article about the state of surveillance technology after the September 11, 2001, attacks, and gave my team at the University of Maryland an interesting task as part of their research.

Tony Mendez was the CIA officer who helped rescue six Americans from the US embassy in Tehran in 1980 by disguising them as a Canadian film crew; the escape was the basis for the 2012 Oscar-winning film *Argo*. Mendez was a master of disguise and often used *Mission Impossible*–style rubber masks, wigs, and fake mustaches to smuggle real-life spies and diplomats out of danger. We were given photos of Mendez taken in both his thirties and his sixties that showed him in various disguises including false teeth and facial markings, in addition to having gained weight when he was older. The challenge was to see whether any facial recognition systems could identify the images. We designed an approach which revealed that while faces from within the same age group matched well despite the disguises, the performance of the system was abysmal when the age difference grew to thirty years.

I received copies of a special edition of the November 2003 *National Geographic* that included our research. A human iris was featured on this cover, while the version designed for the public had the Egyptian pyramids; we were told that the cover art committee was spooked by the iris image. A few months later, I and one of my students, N. Ramanathan, who was working on modeling the aging of facial features for AI, met Mendez at an event at the International Spy Museum in Washington, DC. We took pictures of several of the volunteers before and after he disguised them using wigs, beards, and mustaches to test the accuracy of a facial recognition system we used at that time. Although our system worked perfectly and could identify the people, for fun I told a group of schoolchildren at the museum that our results were secret, just like the work of the spies in the museum.

National Geographic is connected to another story revealing age-related fault lines in recognition software. One of its most famous magazine cover images—in fact, the most recognized photograph in its century-plus history—is a 1984 image by Steve McCurry of a 12-year-old green-eyed Afghan refugee named Sharbat Gula. Following a number of unsuccessful attempts to find Gula and learn more about her story years after the initial encounter in a refugee camp, a team from National Geographic Television found her in the mountains near Tora Bora, Afghanistan. After sixteen years, and given that she was a child when McCurry first met her (facial bone growth in children under 18 can dramatically affect recognition software), he needed to have her identity verified. A facial recognition system used Gula's original photograph for matching, but it couldn't recognize her against new images.

Her identity was finally confirmed by both a forensic sculptor and the inventor of iris-recognition software, University of Cambridge professor John Daugman, and McCurry photographed her once more. McCurry's new image of Gula graced the cover of *National Geographic* in 2001. Twenty years later, in November 2021, this orphaned Afghan refugee, made famous through her haunting eyes—and then newly endangered following the Taliban takeover of her homeland—was granted asylum in Italy. By May of 2022, the Taliban decreed that women must cover themselves from head to toe outside the home, which would have hidden those arresting eyes.

Irises remain one of the most trustworthy physical elements for identification. No amount of disguising, plastic surgery, or age-related facial shapeshifting from sagging muscles or deep wrinkles will change them (that said, I have explored using "signatures" of wrinkles for facial recognition identification software). Each iris is unique—even one person's left and right iris patterns are distinct. And, since their patterns include nothing that could lead to racial or gender biases, their accuracy level is quite high. Although this technology can't yet be used to identify individuals at a distance, it's a tremendous contribution to AI-driven biometrics.

FURTHER READING

"National Geographic: Afghan Girl, A Life Revealed" (interview with Steve McCurry), *Washington Post*, April 10, 2001, https://www.washingtonpost.com/wp-srv/liveonline/02/world/world_mccurry041002.htm.

"Biometrics on the Rise: A Surge in the Use of Iris Recognition Technology," *IDEMIA*, July 26, 2021, https://www.idemia.com/news/biometrics-rise-surge-use-iris-recognition-technology-2021-07-26?export=pdf&post_id=7278&force.

Reuters, "Italy Takes In National Geographic's Green-Eyed 'Afghan Girl,'" November 25, 2021, https://www.reuters.com/world/asia-pacific/italy-takes-national-geographics-green-eyed-afghan-girl-2021-11-25/.

of a nearby building. We experimented with many different approaches based on statistical descriptions and attributes, but unfortunately, the results were inadequate. The overall assessment was that the accuracy of methods developed before 2014 was unsatisfactory, and none were ready for deployment on a large scale. Such is the nature of research; sometimes it provides breakthrough answers, but sometimes it sends you back for further refinements, or changes your course—as in our case in 2012, with the advent of deep learning.

DEEP LEARNING ARRIVES

Before 2012, facial recognition systems were tested on only a few thousand face images and as a result, they did not have the accuracy to be deployed in large-scale applications. But along came the development of the deep neural network, which operates a bit like the human brain to match two images by comparing pixels, edges, or blobs of color, and maps the face to its identity, gender, or age—or all of these parameters.

The foundations for present-day neural networks were laid in 1989 by Yann LeCun, who is now a professor at New York University and chief AI scientist at Facebook's parent company, Meta. LeCun suggested implementing a deep neural network using an optimization algorithm known as back-propagation, short for backward propagation of errors, that automatically extracted features.[9] Before deep learning, the features for classifying digits were hand-crafted based on the underlying physics or geometry. With deep learning, the features are learned from data using backpropagation.

While there were additional neural network efforts in the next decades, they didn't make much impact. UC Berkeley researchers developed an approach based on sparse representations that yielded improved performance on several benchmark datasets. It wasn't until 2012 that a big breakthrough occurred. Alex Krizhevsky, a graduate student of Geoffrey Hinton of the University of Toronto, applied a deeper version of LeCun's original algorithm with some modifications.[10] He also demonstrated significant error reduction for the problem of object recognition using a benchmark dataset known as ImageNet. These two scientists fundamentally changed the field of computer vision, and of facial recognition in particular.

Just as the ImageNet database helped ignite a boom in deep learning–based AI methods for object detection and recognition, two facial databases helped advance the development of facial recognition systems. One is the so-called Faces in the Wild dataset of 13,000 labeled images collected from the Web in 2007 by Erik Learned-Miller's group at the University of Massachusetts, and the second is from the Institute of Automation of the Chinese Academy of Sciences. Today's image databases are significantly larger: the original ImageNet database now contains 14 million tagged images in 20,000 categories, while Google's Open Images contains 9 million images, 80 million annotations, and 600 classes.[11]

In 2014, the Intelligence Advanced Research Projects Activity, a unit within the Office of the Director of National Intelligence, announced a four-year research program known as JANUS. Its goal was to design facial recognition systems that use still and video sequences from subjects who aren't sitting still as in a driver's license photo, but are either moving or in front of a background with uneven lighting. These are known as unconstrained conditions.

While at the University of Maryland, I led a large team of computer vision researchers from Carnegie Mellon University, Columbia University, Rutgers University, SUNY Buffalo, the University of Colorado, Colorado Springs, and the University of Texas at Dallas to build a facial recognition system that would be effective for these unconstrained conditions. Working together, we delivered a series of systems at the end of each phase of the program. The program, which ran from 2014 to 2020, came at the right time. Deep learning–based methods offered the best recognition accuracy as larger datasets of faces became available. Also, the test and evaluation team for the JANUS program provided the means for transforming university-based software into broader commercial software, using what are known as application programming interfaces (APIs). This enabled the JANUS-supported face recognition systems to be easily evaluated by third-party entities, like the test and evaluation team and transition partners in US government laboratories.

A few years ago, however, the issue of bias in the programs

emerged, which has fundamentally altered how academic institutions and tech companies alike design and build facial recognition technology. A 2018 study conducted by researchers at the MIT Media Lab evaluated commercial facial recognition systems from Microsoft, IBM, and the Chinese firm Megvii, on datasets that had faces of light- and dark-skinned females and males.[12] The study found that they didn't perform well on the gender-classification task for dark-skinned females but were quite accurate for light-skinned males. In the experiments, error rates in determining the gender of light-skinned men were never worse than 0.8 percent. For darker-skinned women, however, the error rates exceeded 20 percent in one program and more than 34 percent in the other two. After the study was published, Microsoft and IBM both pledged to improve the accuracy of their programs; the Chinese firm did not respond.[13]

The 2018 study raised questions about how the computer engineers at these firms evaluate and train these algorithms. According to the study, one facial recognition system claimed an accuracy rate of more than 97 percent for its face recognition system. But the photo dataset used to assess its performance was more than 77 percent male and more than 83 percent white. In addition, a 2019 study by researchers at the University of Colorado found that commercially available facial recognition systems fared poorly when tasked with identifying non-binary or transgender individuals.[14]

These studies created a major concern among facial recognition researchers and many advocacy groups. The bias found in face recognition systems has raised calls for a moratorium on deploying such systems; it has also pushed efforts to regulate this technology at the federal, state, and local levels. In 2020, IBM abandoned its facial recognition business, citing the problem of racially biased surveillance.[15] Microsoft and Amazon paused sales of their face recognition engines to law enforcement, but in 2022 both firms unveiled new programs they say are more accurate. At the same time, the US government has worked to improve the accuracy of its facial recognition systems, including the JANUS program that my group helped develop. Still, there are no federal regulations or standards in place governing these systems and their accuracy, and no federal agencies regulate their use. With a lack of federal guidelines on facial recognition, local officials in Virginia, Massachusetts, and Maine and more than a dozen US cities (including Portland, San Francisco, and Baltimore, which I'll discuss later in the chapter) have banned or restricted the technology's use by public officials or police.

A 2019 review of facial recognition algorithms by the National Institute of Standards and Technology—an agency that reviews and sets operating standards for various forms of technology used by government agencies and commercial firms—found that Asian and African American individuals were up to 100 times more likely to be misidentified than white men, depending on the particular algorithm and type of search applied. Native Americans had the highest false-positive rate of all ethnicities, according to the study, which found that the accuracy of systems developed by a variety of companies differed widely.[16] Three Black men—two in Detroit and one in New Jersey—were arrested for crimes they did not commit using flawed facial recognition technology, according to the *New York Times*. Two are suing the local police departments that used the systems.[17]

Despite these problems—and the subsequent fixes and patches put into place by tech companies—the field continues to grow each year. A 2021 report by the Government Accountability Office (GAO) found that 10 federal agencies expect to increase their use of facial recognition systems by 2023.[18] The agencies use face-scanning technology so that employees can unlock their phones and laptops or access buildings, although some also use it to track people and investigate crime. Department of Agriculture staffers told the GAO that the department wants to use the technology to monitor live surveillance feeds at its facilities to send an alert if it spots any faces found on a watch list.

Facial recognition systems in some sectors are improving. In 2021, researchers at NIST tested 29 commercial facial recognition systems used by airlines to identify passengers before boarding an airplane.[19] The seven top-performing algorithms successfully identified at least 99.5 percent of passengers, while the most accurate algorithm was accurate 99.87 percent of the time. Accuracy improved when the systems were able to use more than one image of the passenger. Perhaps most importantly, the NIST team found that for the more accurate algorithms "error rates are so low that accuracy variations across sex and race are insignificant." The NIST study is good news for air travelers, and the results show that the accuracy of facial recognition technology can be improved. At the same time, it's clear that some algorithms shouldn't be used on the public.

CONSCIOUS AND UNCONSCIOUS BIASES

When my Johns Hopkins colleague Carlos Castillo, associate research professor of electrical and computer engineering, began his doctoral studies in 2005, he told people that he worked in facial recognition. "The first comment I was given in response was often: 'That's never going to work.' Now, the first comment I get is, 'Oh, those systems are biased,'" Castillo says. "The conversation has evolved."

Castillo says that the people he meets often have mixed opinions about the use of facial recognition. People realize that they'll probably interact with it in some form in their day-to-day lives, but at the same time, many worry about the risks of misidentification and the invasiveness of surveillance.

Castillo notes that bias can occur in object recognition, too—a branch of artificial intelligence in which an algorithm

Protecting Intellectual Property

Between the trials, errors, and victories of lab and field research and its applications in AI programs and devices comes the patent application process to secure intellectual property. This can take years, as the work is first presented to a university or company (and their attorneys) to persuade them to invest in the registration, which can be a bit of a kabuki dance—you're never sure what will click with them. It then moves forward to the US Patent and Trademark Office, whose experts verify the science and check it against that in other granted patents—which sometimes means they'll ask you to further differentiate your work from other claims. In case you're curious: no, artificial intelligence programs cannot be listed as inventors on patents, even if their machine learning created the solution. According to a 2021 BBC article, there's a "long-running battle to grant machines the status of inventor,"[1] but so far, the courts—at least in the United States and the United Kingdom—aren't having it.

Once notification of the patent's grant is received, it's both a relief and a thrill. As an engineer, you feel like you've built something that people believe has value, which is satisfying for you and your team. Your invention may go on to assist other researchers who will invent even more solutions, and it may also eventually offer anything from convenience to safety to communities worldwide. On a lighter note, it's the fantasy of every owner that their patent will be used without permission in a major commercial, industrial, or defense application; infringement can bring a massive payday!

The first of eight patents that include my and my co-inventors' research is US Patent No. 7,184,071, "Method of Three-Dimensional Object Reconstruction from a Video Sequence Using a Generic Model," which was issued in 2007. The technology's method creates a three-dimensional image from a video's two-dimensional images. This work received a surprising amount of attention, including a 2005 Associated Press story that was syndicated by four hundred media outlets around the world.

Another of my facial recognition patents is US Patent No. 10,860,837, "Deep Multi-Task Learning Framework for Face Detection, Landmark Localization, Pose Estimation, and Gender Recognition," which was issued in 2020. One of my co-inventors at the University of Maryland was Rajeev Ranjan, who was then a graduate student, and is now a senior applied scientist at Amazon. The moment he shared how the HyperFace algorithm outperformed the existing face-preprocessing techniques we were using, I was so happy—and proud of him. This was a major breakthrough toward securing the top spot in the IARPA JANUS project mentioned on page 75.

For anyone who'd like an inside view on an AI patent's components, Rajeev has provided a description of one of the invention's supporting figures, and two of its equations.

The figure shows the neural network model used in the HyperFace algorithm. Given an input image, the model predicts the presence of a face; the 3D head pose rotation of the face; the location of associated landmarks such as eye centers, nose tip, and mouth corners; the

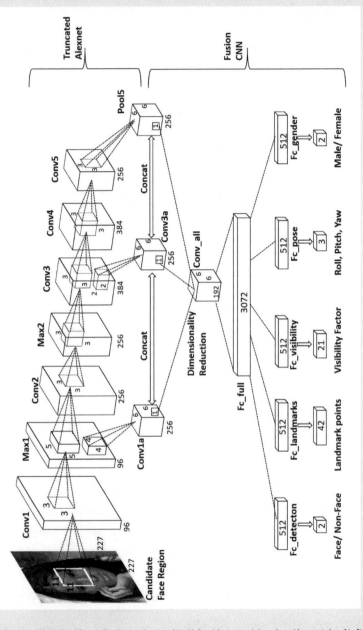

The architecture of the proposed HyperFace. Courtesy Rajeev Ranjan

visibility of the predicted landmarks; and whether the face belongs to a male or a female. In order to train this model, we apply five different loss functions, one for each task mentioned above. Here's a short description of two of these loss functions along with their equations.

Face Detection Loss: We use binary cross-entropy loss to train the face detection task. Given an input image I, binary face label l_D ($l_D = 1$ if image is a face, 0 otherwise), and the face detection softmax probability p_D (obtained from the model), the binary cross-entropy loss is defined as:

$$loss_p = -(1 - l_D) * \log(1 - p_D) - l_D * \log(p_D)$$

Pose Estimation Loss: We use mean-squared error loss to train the pose estimation task. Given an input face image I the 3D head pose rotation angles: p^1, p^2, and p^3 corresponding to the pitch, yaw, and roll, and the predicted head pose angles: $p\hat{}_1$, $p\hat{}_2$, and $p\hat{}_3$ obtained from the model, the pose estimation loss is given by:

$$loss_p = 1/3 \ ((p_1 - p\hat{}_1)^2 + (p_2 - p\hat{}_2)^2 + (p_3 - p\hat{}_3)^2)$$

FURTHER READING

"AI Cannot Be the Inventor of a Patent, Appeals Court Rules," *BBC News*, September 23, 2021, https://www.bbc.com/news/technology-58668534.

and camera identify images taken from surroundings or the internet. Just like facial recognition, object recognition has taken a big leap since the arrival of deep neural networks. This is vital not only for the development of both robotics and automated vehicles, but also for search engines and apps that evaluate and tag online images. But gender bias is present here, too: In recent years general online searches for "doctors" turn up men, while searches for "nurses" turn up women.[20]

"If you let these systems have free rein, they will learn and lock into the biases that are out there," Castillo says. "This takes corrective action. You need to tell the network that being female and dressed in white is not a predictor for being a nurse. Or being white and male is not a predictor for being a doctor. Those affirmative observations need to be given to the network." One solution to fighting this bias is greater diversity in the images used for training algorithms for object and facial recognition in tandem with greater diversity in the humans who are programming them. This must begin with increasing diversity in faculty and student recruitment.

Charles Isbell, the Georgia Tech computer scientist, has thought about this issue of bias in artificial intelligence and facial recognition programs and says that it isn't realistic to eliminate it. "The goal is not to get rid of bias, it's to make certain that you know you're aware of your bias," Isbell says. "Bias is not something you can get rid of. It's something you manage, and you're aware of, and then you act accordingly."[21]

In public writings, conferences, and media posts, Isbell has been pushing companies and academic institutions to do better when it comes to recruiting, hiring, and promoting a more diverse pool of AI developers and computer engineers. Without a greater mix of backgrounds and experiences by the people who program AI algorithms, AI agents will continue to come up with biased outputs. "What computers are better at than anything that we've ever been able to build in the entire history of human time is making us so much more efficient," he says. "It doesn't care what it is we're doing, it just makes us more efficient. So, it's only going to amplify our biases."

Meanwhile, as the use of facial recognition expands, private citizens, developers, and some companies are urging Congress to promulgate laws regulating the industry. In June 2021, a group of Democratic lawmakers proposed a moratorium on almost any use of facial recognition by any government agency.[22] President Joe Biden appointed Princeton University professor Alondra Nelson—a sociologist who studies the intersections of science and race—as deputy director of the White House Office of Science and Technology Policy. She is now tasked with making public recommendations to reduce the problem of algorithm bias, although the administration doesn't have a formal position on the use of facial recognition.[23] The OSTP completed a public comment period on the issue of facial recognition bias in January 2022 and was expected to issue its final report sometime in 2022.[24]

USE AND MISUSE IN BALTIMORE

One politician who's trying to make a difference is Maryland state senator Charles E. Sydnor III. For years, Sydnor had been advocating for restrictions on police use of facial recognition. But then in 2015 the issue came to a head during the violent protests in Baltimore over the death of Freddie Gray, a young Black man who died of a spinal cord injury after spending several hours being driven around unsecured in the back of a police van. The medical examiner ruled the death a homicide, but trials resulted in acquittal of the police officers, dropped charges, and a mistrial. During subsequent public protests in Baltimore, police set up facial recognition systems throughout the city to identify individuals with prior records or outstanding warrants. Civil rights advocates said the police tactics were a form of surveillance that violated the constitutional protection against unlawful search and seizure. Since the incident, the Baltimore City Council has restricted the use of facial recognition by private companies and city agencies, although the police department was exempted from the new law because of strong opposition by its union.

Sydnor sees both sides of the debate. Some of his constituents like the idea of greater scrutiny of their neighborhoods, which have been plagued by high crime rates in recent years. Others complain that facial recognition systems unfairly target low-income minority neighborhoods, in addition to the false positive recognition issues in communities of color. In the years since the protests and the police tactics involving facial recognition, Sydnor introduced legislation to ban or curtail its use.

But after the January 6, 2021, insurrection at the US Capitol, his position shifted. "I've moved along the spectrum," Sydnor says. "When I was initially looking at it, I may have been leaning more to the ban. But after what happened on January 6, the initial urge was, 'I hope they had facial recognition.' I understand the utility."[25] Federal law enforcement officials identified hundreds of lawbreakers at the Capitol by scanning social media posts as well as publicly available videos. Many others were turned in through a kind of crowdsourced human face recognition campaign in which volunteers took video screen grabs of rioters, used commercially available face-matching systems, and sent tips to law enforcement officials.[26] The *New York Times* reported that the FBI sent images of Capitol rioters to local and state police departments, which then used facial recognition to match the faces with images in existing databases.[27]

When Baltimore authorities used facial recognition to scan for lawbreakers during the Freddie Gray riots, their system matched faces with images in databases containing government-provided photos, such as driver's license photos and mug shots. But to identify US Capitol rioters, federal agents used an app from Clearview AI, a privately held firm founded by Hoan Ton-That, an Australian entrepreneur, and Richard

Schwartz, a former New York City councilmember. The firm built a system that has collected more than 20 billion images from social media networks and other public websites. When an officer runs a search, the app quickly provides links to social media and internet sites where the person's face has appeared. The firm has been sued by groups such as the ACLU, immigrants' rights groups and others concerned that Clearview's program violates their constitutional right to privacy.[28] At the same time, Clearview says it's expanding its customer base from law enforcement to banks and other private businesses.[29] In the weeks after the Capitol riot, several hundred protesters were charged, however the FBI's Most Wanted website continued to ask the public for help to identify video clips and images of dozens of rioters in 2022.[30]

Given the events of January 6, 2021, Sydnor believes that police should be able to use facial recognition technology to identify lawbreakers. Passing an outright ban isn't possible because of opposition from law enforcement at the local and federal level. But he believes that limits are needed, for example, against using the technology to allow police to establish probable cause for a crime that may be planned but hasn't occurred or as the sole piece of evidence used to convict a suspect. "We're in the wild, wild west, and there's really no regulation," Sydnor says about facial recognition. "It's been used for such a long time that trying to put that genie back in the bottle can be quite difficult."

To develop solutions, Sydnor set up a working group of academic experts, legal advisers, civil rights advocates, police officers, and technology-industry representatives who met twice a month in 2021. The group came up with a compromise bill requiring yearly audits of the police use of facial recognition, and limited its use in criminal proceedings. It also required the state's Department of Public Safety and Correctional Services to adopt a model policy to train police how to use it. After a public hearing in March 2022, the bill was still awaiting a committee vote in the Maryland State Legislature.

Still, Sydnor says he's optimistic that in time, the legislation will pass and it could serve as a model for other states. He says that regulations are trying to catch up with a technology that is already being used by police and others. "We lawmakers are behind the curve," Sydnor says. "Technology moves at a lot quicker pace than we do."

THE FUTURE OF FACIAL RECOGNITION

Where do we go now and what will we make of facial recognition technology? As a researcher, I find the issues inherent in facial recognition a challenging one. The performance of facial recognition systems is quite good in some circumstances, such as when using driver's licenses or passports to check visitors at a building entrance or at an airport checkpoint. The performance of face recognition systems that exist today, however, is not good enough when faces are at distances of several hundred yards and beyond or when the cameras are positioned on a building's roof. Also, the performance drops when a range of ages or races is involved. While my own and other groups have developed methods that can handle a span of 10 years or less (as is the case for passport renewal), when the gap is 30 years or more, the algorithm's performance drops considerably. The issue of bias must be addressed. My team and others are working hard to develop methods for reducing bias that involves gender and skin tone. Facial recognition systems specifically, and biometrics systems in general, can be fooled by presentation attacks. For example, someone can wear a mask that looks like my face and try to fool an access control system. I agree with Senator Sydnor that much research needs to be done to address all these challenges before these recognition systems can be widely deployed.

A FORCE FOR GOOD

Facial recognition software is a critical strategic tool that's used to help prevent child sex trafficking by scanning millions of online sex ads and matching them with reports of missing minors in the United States.[31] International airports use facial recognition to make sure the person who dropped off their bag is the same one checking onto the airplane.[32] US Customs and Border Protection officials have deployed facial recognition kiosks at select airports to speed entry for preselected, low-risk passengers entering the United States after international flights, a program known a Global Entry.[33] In a 2021 passenger survey, the International Air Transport Association found that 73 percent of passengers are willing to share their biometric data to improve airport processes, up from 46 percent in 2019. For many travelers, your face is now your passport, as the *New York Times* reports.[34]

At Kansas State University, a team of researchers is working on applying facial recognition algorithms to cows so that they can be tracked in the event of an animal disease outbreak.[35] There are many other interesting applications of the technologies, but the current discussion over privacy and bias is focused on the public use of facial recognition.

While technology focused on identifying faces has dominated conversations about privacy, security, and bias, many related technologies have also been under development. For example, the idea of identifying someone by the way they walk, the so-called gait signature, has been touted as a technology for remote identification of humans at security checkpoints. Supported by DARPA as part of its program on Human Identification at Distance (HID), my team at the University of Maryland, College Park developed a method for gait-based human identification.[36] Our algorithm, and others developed by other participants in the HID program, were tested on relatively small datasets and did not get deployed in full applications. In a new IARPA project known as BRIAR, the Hopkins team, including Carlos Castillo and Vishal Patel will be revisiting this research to investigate if methods based on deep neural networks will be more accurate for identifying humans at distance. Although gait has been an intriguing feature for identification, it was not discriminative enough for deployment. But, it might be used to screen potentially dangerous individuals to see if something heavy might be strapped to their ankles or torso, which would affect their walk. It may also assist in detection of diseases with motion-related issues, like Parkinson's.

Other algorithms for remote surveillance include face recognition at distances up to 1,000 yards. While we worked on addressing a version of this problem for shorter distances from 2008 to 2013, this issue is gaining renewed attention due to improvements with cameras and deep-learning performance. In our preliminary studies, we've found that faces are hard to detect at 1,000 yards due to atmospheric turbulence and degradations in the clarity of the face image. This is challenging due to changes in postures and, sometimes, changes in clothing. This problem has received considerable attention over the years and we will continue to work on ways to solve it.

Artificial intelligence has tremendous potential to promote an equitable world. AI can give us explanations for complicated decisions, and we can analyze those explanations and learn from them. Computers and humans can work together well and have complementary sets of skills. That's the idealistic view. But in the real world, people—including computer engineers and software programmers—have both conscious and unconscious biases. This means that the algorithms they're designing may also be embedded with those same biases. The way to eliminate bias and errors is to improve the technology, and improve the diversity of scholars, researchers, and programmers. The way to prevent privacy violations is to work with policymakers to draft guidelines for its use rather than ban or eliminate it. I feel strongly about this, because there are so many ways that this technology can help people.

CHAPTER 4

The Promise of Autonomous Vehicles

ERNST DICKMANNS REMEMBERED sitting inside a van as it accelerated through empty stretches of the autobahn in his native Bavaria. Dickmanns, a former German spacecraft engineer turned professor, had been recruited by German carmaker Daimler-Benz in 1986 to build a self-driving vision-guided vehicle that could eventually be sold to the public. "It was a strange feeling the first time I got into [it] . . . it was a five-ton van," Dickmanns told an interviewer for an oral history project in 2010.[1] "And when this accelerates like a human driver, really, with all its power it has, for the first 10 minutes, you are very anxious [about] what's going to happen, and then you see, well, [it] behaves like a human behaves, and you get accustomed to it."

The first phase of Dickmanns's project was focused on transforming the boxy Mercedes van into a rolling scientific workshop. The professor and his team of engineers crammed it with video cameras, range-finding sensors, and state-of-the-art computers that would control the van's steering wheel, gas pedal, and brakes. Software translated the video image data into driving commands using an Intel 8086 16-bit computer chip that was unable to capture the entire image of the road in front of the van. This forced the engineers to devise a method in which they divided the video screen into 12 boxes, and were able to load enough pixels to get several of the boxes filled with the image. As each frame of the video moved along, the team members were able to switch to a different set of windows, giving a spotty, but ultimately useful view of the road to the computer driving the vehicle. Despite these obstacles, Dickmanns's engineering achievement was remarkable: creating the equivalent of the Model T for autonomous vehicles.

Instead of relying on electronic signals embedded in the highway that would communicate with the vehicle as some previous efforts had done, his team of engineers from the Bundeswehr University Munich designed a computer vision program that could rapidly identify obstacles using video cameras and translate the data into driving commands (the US Army was also developing a computer vision program for a robotic truck at around this time). Dickmanns's team continued to progress on its little-known Prometheus project, which culminated in a stunning public demonstration in October 1994 when they took the self-driving technology they'd developed from the van and installed it in a pair of S-Class Mercedes SEL 500 sedans. On a sunny, clear morning, the engineers picked up a group of VIPs from Charles de Gaulle Airport in Paris, drove them to Autoroute 1, and switched the two cars into self-driving mode on the highway. Over the next few days, the robot cars drove in traffic at speeds up to 130 kilometers (81 miles) per hour, changing lanes and settling into a convoy of sorts through the outskirts of Paris. At least one engineer kept his hands on the steering wheel in case something went wrong—but the cars were doing the driving. "Sometimes, we would take our hands off the wheel," remembers Reinhold Behringer, one of the engineers who sat in the driver's seat during the demonstration.[2] The demonstration wasn't perfect, but it proved that a car could be driven autonomously. "It was a test," said Behringer. "When, for instance, there was a car in front of us that covered up the road markings, and on the other side, the markings were washed away, then the lane identification feature had a problem."

But that demonstration of German automotive technology wasn't enough for the ambitious engineers. A year later, Dickmanns's team took another vehicle all the way from Bavaria to Denmark, with the self-driving car hitting more than 175 kilometers (109 miles) per hour. Yet despite the spectacular engineering successes of Dickmanns's team of researchers, the project sputtered to a halt a few years later after Daimler pulled its funding. "It was an interesting concept," Behringer told a reporter for *Politico* in 2018.[3] "But for many it was still way too futuristic."

For years, Ernst Dickmanns's work was nearly forgotten. But the story of his self-driving Mercedes sedans was in some ways a Sputnik moment for autonomous cars—an achievement that was light-years ahead of what had come before and that paved the way for future research projects. But it also reflected one of the persistent truths of such vehicles: The existing technology is still behind what commercial automakers have been promising the public for decades. As I write this in 2022—after tens of billions of dollars have been invested by tech firms and academic labs alike over the past decade—motorists are still waiting for Dickmanns's dream to come true. The promise of a self-driving car, while not fulfilled yet, has contributed to the installation of many features in modern cars that make the everyday driving experience safer and more enjoyable. Even entry-level cars have features such as alerts for blind spots and when changing lanes, collision avoidance systems, and pedestrian detection systems. I expect this trend to continue.

Even though we probably won't see fully autonomous passenger cars at a dealer's showroom anytime soon, a growing number of limited-use autonomous-driving situations—hauling cargo, delivering airport passengers, and self-driving taxis in well-mapped areas, for example—are slowly becoming the proving ground for both commercial success and passenger safety.

FROM THE PENTAGON TO
NO HANDS ACROSS AMERICA

From Dickmanns's mid-1980s experiments with German vans to today's hands-free electric battery–powered Tesla, the evolution of autonomy on the road has come a long way. It was spurred and developed, as many technologies are, by the military. Around the same time that Dickmanns and his crew were developing that Mercedes van in Germany, the Pentagon created its autonomous land vehicle (ALV) program. On May 31, 1985, a 10-foot-tall, blue-and-white vehicle crept along a dirt road outside of Denver at around 3 miles per hour.[4] A large roof-mounted, closed-circuit camera peeked out from the top of its boxy frame while three diesel engines powered the ALV, which was assembled by defense contractor Martin Marietta with components provided by several Pentagon-funded technology developers, including the Hughes Research Lab, Carnegie Mellon University (CMU), and the University of Maryland. No driver was inside, but the ALV carried six full racks of electronic equipment in dust-free, air-conditioned comfort. The ALV was created in nine months. As computing power became more powerful and efficiently sized, the engineering team behind the ALV was able to transfer its algorithms into smaller computer kits that were capable of converting existing military trucks into semi-autonomous vehicles, according to a history of the ALV by Lockheed Martin.[5] After several iterations, the ALV evolved into the Squad Mission Support System (SMSS), an autonomous vehicle that could carry a ton of military gear over rocky trails. The SMSS made its debut in Afghanistan in 2011.

As that first-generation ALV crawled across a Rocky Mountain road to simulate combat terrain, in Pittsburgh, a DARPA-funded team at CMU began working on a project to build a self-navigating vehicle that could follow paved roads and city traffic—a vehicle that regular folks rather than soldiers would someday use.

The CMU Navigation Laboratory team converted a Pontiac minivan that lumbered along at a few miles per hour, remembers Chuck Thorpe, a former CMU professor who directed the research group that developed the first vehicle in 1989. It was so slow because the computers in the late 1980s needed enough time to process visual information from cameras and other sensors.

"You could fire up the system, walk off and get a cup of coffee and come back and [the vehicle] hadn't moved all that far, but it was still moving," Thorpe says.[6] The image processing was slower than the changes to the scene around it. "You'd have to worry about things like the sun going behind the clouds. Not only does the sky get dimmer but colors change. Instead of bright yellow sunlight you maybe now have grayish colors underneath the trees."

Thorpe says that CMU and Dickmanns's group developed a competition of sorts in the late 1980s and early 1990s as they broke new ground in automation technology. They compared notes at meetings and conferences that they both attended.

"There are lots of different ways of approaching computer vision," Thorpe says, adding that Dickmanns "had a very German way of approaching it, where he was going to build a mathematical model of the vehicle, the steering mechanism and the German roads—and [it] was all highly tuned and worked quite well if you had his vehicle on German roads. But it turns out that roads in the United States are all higgledy-piggledy, more than in Germany, and don't always follow the same nice conventions, and so we had to be able to adapt to a much wider variety of things than the autobahn. We learned from him, he learned from us, and it was a good-natured rivalry."

In the hills around Pittsburgh, Thorpe and his colleagues were experimenting with various vehicles using off-the-shelf video cameras and computers that they adapted to make the vehicle see its surroundings. One of the biggest challenges was getting all the electronic equipment inside, he remembers.

"To really make a difference, you have to have a big enough vehicle that it can carry the computers, the sensors, the power supply, and the graduate students," Thorpe says. "Computers filled up racks and racks of electronics and we had a 20-kilowatt generator from a fire engine. Importantly, we had room on board for four or five graduate students. And that made for great teamwork and great camaraderie, and if something didn't work right and you say oh, we hadn't considered that was a possibility, well let's change this bit in your software and this bit in my software, recompile it, and see if it'll work."

It took a while, but by July 1995, the CMU team had been through several iterations, and the Navlab 5 vehicle was ready for a serious road test. Thorpe remembers that the Pittsburgh team had wanted to see a new automated electronic highway system that the California Department of Transportation had installed in some of the freeways to help future self-driving cars navigate. It worked by embedding small electronic sensors that would communicate directly with receivers on each car. The embedded sensors would tell the vehicle sensors about traffic jams and weather events up the road and help the driver make better decisions. Known as the Intelligent Vehicle Highway System, the concept was developed by the US Department of Transportation in the early 1990s and promised motorists a completely automated highway experience.[7] Congress never appropriated enough money to get it off the ground, and the program was never fully implemented. But in 1995, California had a few test sensors set up as a demonstration, and Thorpe's team decided to take Navlab 5 to San Diego. Thorpe stayed behind and monitored daily reports from his lab while a crew took the Pontiac on a cross-country odyssey that turned out to be a big media success. That was perhaps because of its name No Hands Across America or because at nearly 3,000 miles, it was the longest trip by a self-driving vehicle in history (although Navlab passengers operated the gas pedal and brakes).[8]

"We learned a lot about the different kinds of roads that you encounter as you go across states. We learned a lot about the vagaries of highway departments, things like new pavement in Kansas at night with no lines painted on it. There are places where they let people drive, and they haven't bothered to paint the lines on yet. You better be able to cope with situations like that."

CMU's Navigation Laboratory continued building self-driving vehicles until the early 2000s, modifying Pontiac Bonnevilles, Oldsmobile Silhouettes, transit buses from Houston, and finally the Navlab 11, a Jeep Wrangler.[9] In recent years, the Navlab has pivoted to designing smart transportation infrastructure, focusing on machine vision applications and affordable sensors. In 2014, the lab developed a system to monitor how road conditions deteriorate over time, using images or videos collected by smartphones mounted in cabs, garbage trucks, police cars, or delivery trucks that already make regular rounds on city roads for other purposes.[10] The city of Pittsburgh has been piloting the program, along with systems to ease traffic flow.[11]

VISION FOR VEHICLES

I first became interested in self-driving car technologies in 1993, when I was a member of the collaborative research team from the University of Maryland, the University of Pennsylvania, and the University of Rochester that won a DARPA contract to develop algorithms for reconnaissance, search, and target acquisition. DARPA tasked us with developing technologies to support unmanned ground vehicles that were outfitted with stereo cameras, an infrared camera, and a system known as laser detection and ranging (LADAR) that can sense human-made objects. Data collected from these vehicles were given to us for processing. In addition to sensor data, metadata such as the position of vehicles were made available. The goals were to develop algorithms for detecting and tracking objects and pedestrians while the vehicle was in motion.

Before this project, computer vision researchers like myself used still images or videos collected by stationary cameras and then processed the data. The big jump during this experiment was to process data from multiple sensors on the vehicle in real time.

Back then, we didn't have enough computing power, but engineers at Princeton's SRI, hired by DARPA, developed a work-around with a special-purpose video supercomputer they called the Princeton Engine.[12] We also had to compensate for the vehicle's motion while attempting to detect vehicles, obstacles, and humans around it. We had to develop real-time methods to compensate for shifts in video frames due to vehicle motion in order to address what's known as the video stabilization problem. Once the video frames from a vehicle's cameras were stabilized, you could stitch them together to create a panoramic mosaic that yields a complete view of the collected data. A simplified version of this capability, the digital image stabilization option, became available for video camcorders much later and is now standard for many devices, including Apple's iPhone. My team's contribution was developing algorithms for video stabilization and for detecting and tracking stationary objects such as buildings, as well as those in motion such as pedestrians, cyclists, and perhaps a runaway pet using computer vision technologies. We demonstrated the effectiveness of these algorithms, which can estimate quantities like time-to-contact and time-to-synchronization; these are the basic tasks that a self-driving car must know how to assess.

One of the related problems that the US Army was interested in was knowing when the terrain around a vehicle drops so that a self-driving jeep, tank, or armored personnel carrier could be stopped or rerouted. We developed several algorithms to do this by converting the estimated displacements in video frames due to vehicle motion to depth maps. Negative depth maps were good indicators of terrain depths and even potholes, which can cause vehicles and robots to get stuck. Many of these problems were efficiently solved by the researchers recruited by DARPA. Engineers at the NASA Jet Propulsion Laboratory in Pasadena, California also developed many elegant solutions for these tasks as demonstrated later by the Mars Rover program.

The DARPA programs for unmanned ground vehicles motivated computer vision and robotics researchers to look at solutions for navigating the vehicles in urban environments, on battlefields, and on freeways. DARPA's initial work on unmanned ground vehicles, which began in 1985 with the ALV program,[13] laid the foundation for unmanned aerial vehicles (UAVs), also known as drones. The first such drone, known as Amber, took flight in 1988.[14] Amber was followed by the Predator. I recall that videos collected by aerial vehicles such as the Predator were made available to us as part of DARPA programs known as Image Understanding for Battlefield Awareness (IUBA) and Video Surveillance and Monitoring (VSAM). For these programs, my students developed algorithms for video stabilization, object detection, and tracking algorithms using radar images, infrared, and video frames. The culminating event of this program was an impressive demonstration done at CMU that showed how information collected by UAVs and ground-based cameras can be fused to create a robust awareness of what was happening in an environment.

Other programs in the late 1990s asked research teams to focus on detecting activities such as someone stealing a car and driving it away, or detecting whether a small group of people might be assembling a missile launcher, launching a missile, and then packing out and disappearing. Some of these Pentagon-funded drone technologies are now being used by commercial firms; you might soon see them being applied to pizza delivery on your driveway using a drone. In fact, drones have already been used to rush medicine to remote areas.

RACE ACROSS THE DESERT

By the early 2000s, DARPA was considering new ways to spur technological development instead of simply funding another academic lab on a three- or five-year grant cycle. Anthony Tether, who was the DARPA director at the time, came up with the idea of a public "challenge" that would have a $1 million prize, provided by funds from Congress. The challenge had to fulfill two requirements: It had to have a low barrier of entry that would make it possible for anyone with an engineering background to build a robot car, and it had to pass the "grand-mother test" of having an easy-to-discern winner rather than relying on a complicated set of metrics and scientific data to determine the victor. Thus was born the first DARPA Grand Challenge: a robot car race in the Mojave Desert that would occur in March 2004. A few teams were expected to compete, but when Tether and deputy program manager Thomas Strat showed up at the Petersen Automotive Museum in downtown Los Angeles for an open house a few months before the event, more than 500 people had lined up outside the door.[15]

Although 104 teams applied to enter the contest, Strat says, during a field trial in early March at the California Speedway in Fontana, he and his DARPA colleagues narrowed the field down to 15 vehicles that could be operated safely.

The idea was that each fully autonomous vehicle—without remote controls or driver—would travel through the desert to reach a set of waypoints over 142 miles. The race drew intense media coverage, from CNN and PBS to the *New York Times* and *Scientific American*,[16] but the final result was less impressive than many expected. *Popular Science* headlined its coverage: "DARPA's Debacle in the Desert."[17] The teams were composed of undergraduate engineering students from various universities and industry partners. Ohio State University and Oshkosh Trucking put together a 32,000-pound six-wheel military truck that got stuck in some bushes. Auburn University's SciAutonics II dropped out of the running at mile 6.7, its Israeli dune buggy stuck in an embankment. Digital Auto Drive quit at mile 6.0, its Toyota Tundra stymied by a football-size rock. The Golem Group from UCLA stopped at mile 5.2, its pickup stalled on a hill with insufficient throttle to move forward. Team Caltech, another race favorite, dropped out at mile 1.3, its Chevy Tahoe SUV having careened off course and through a fence. A modified Honda Acura MDX assembled by the Palos Verdes High School Road Warriors aborted when the vehicle lurched right immediately after start-up and headed for the grandstands until DARPA hit the disabling "E-Stop" button. CMU's winning vehicle, "Sandstorm," traveled only 7.4 miles before running off the road and catching fire.[18]

AI in Contemporary Warfare

Armed forces throughout history have deployed cutting-edge inventions and technologies to defeat their enemies. For decades, the US military has funded artificial intelligence research to create battlefield advantages for its soldiers, sailors, and pilots. Today, nearly every military force in the world has adopted applications of AI, including vehicle and weaponry applications, facial recognition, and deepfake videos. These demoralize the opposing force's troops, enhance rapid decision-making capacities, keep distance between human operators and their missile strikes, and elevate intelligence-gathering capabilities.

With its bloody tank battles, shelling of civilians, and the resistance's use of Molotov cocktails, Russia's recent invasion of Ukraine can seem more like a conflict from World War I or II than a contemporary series of battles. Yet both sides also deploy equipment with AI-based technologies alongside those century-old methods to gain tactical advantages. Some are of the most advanced and brutal weapons in their updated arsenals are bomb-transporting drones.

Russia launched a "suicide drone" on the battlefield that uses artificial intelligence, rather than a human operator, to identify targets, although humans are still behind strike decisions. With a wingspan of four feet, the sleek Russian-made KUB-BLA drone resembles a small fighter jet, travels up to 30 minutes, then crashes into a target with a small explosive, according to a report in *Wired,* enough to destroy a tank. The device's manufacturer claims it features "intelligent detection and recognition of objects by class and type in real time."

In March 2022, the US equipped Ukrainian forces with 700 Aero-Vironment, Inc. Switchblade "kamikazes"—one-way, unmanned aerial vehicles outfitted with cameras, guidance systems, and explosives that are guided by a human operator watching a video feed. These drones can be programmed to automatically strike targets miles away and can be steered around obstacles until the time is right to strike. Switchblades can fly for 40 minutes and up to 50 miles. According to *Bloomberg,* these dive-bombing, antiarmor, warhead-loaded "tank killers" are operated using a tablet-based touchscreen fire-control system with the option to pilot the loitering missile manually.

The Ukrainian war also saw the debut of the Phoenix Ghost from California's AEVEX Aerospace that's deployed against armored ground units. This drone was fast-tracked for the Air Force; it was active in combat as a field test before it appeared on AEVEX's website. Like the Switchblade, it's light and portable (it can fit in a backpack)—but it can fly and hover (or "loiter" as they say) six times longer.

In addition, Ukraine's Territorial Defense forces include drone operators—some of whom until recently were only drone enthusiasts, but are now documenting war crimes, including attacks on cultural institutions like churches and museums, and against unarmed civilians.

Whether for surgical strikes or intelligence gathering, drones are recognized as such a vital component of the resistance that Ukrainian artist Taras Borovok recorded a folk song about the Turkish-made Bayraktar TB2 drone, which has gone viral. Borovok likens the drone to a "diligent shepherd" that drives tanks back. There are also songs praising the American anti-tank Javelins.

In addition to AI-driven transport weaponry, Ukraine's military used

Clearview AI's facial recognition technology, the same software used by US law enforcement to track the January 6, 2021, Capitol rioters in Washington, DC, to help identify dead Russian soldiers and secure checkpoints, according to a report by Reuters. Clearview, a privately held US firm, did not provide its smartphone app-based software to Russia. Their officials collected more than 2 billion images from the Russian social media service VKontakte using its AI algorithm. These images help Ukrainian officials identify the dead more easily than trying to match fingerprints, and the technology works even if there is facial damage.

Psychological warfare is a tried-and-true and infectious component of conflicts, so it's no surprise that artificial intelligence is deployed for disinformation tools as well. Facebook and YouTube took down a crude "deepfake" video purporting to show Ukraine's president, Volodomyr Zelensky, surrendering to Russia in March 2022. While that video wasn't especially sophisticated, it was widely circulated on the Russian-language version of Telegram and Facebook equivalent, VKontakte. A second video of Russian president Vladimir Putin declaring peace was circulated on Twitter but was considered more satire than misinformation.

FURTHER READING

Paresh Dave and Jeffrey Dastin, "Exclusive: Ukraine Has Started Using Clearview's Facial Recognition during War," Reuters, March 14, 2022. https://www.reuters.com /technology/exclusive-ukraine-has-started-using-clearview-ais-facial-recognition -during -war-2022-03-13/.

Ken Dilanian, Dan DeLuce and Courtney Kube, "Biden Admin Will Provide Ukraine with Killer Drones Called Switchblades," *NBC News.com,* March 15, 2022. https://www .nbcnews.com/politics/national-security/ukraine-asks -biden-admin-armed-drones -jamming-gear-surface-air-missile-rcna20197.

Will Knight, "Russia's Killer Drone in Ukraine Raises Fears of AI in Warfare," *Wired,* March 17, 2022, https://www.wired.com/story/ai-drones-russia-ukraine/.

Reuters Fact Check, "Doctored Video Appears to Show Putin Announcing Peace," Reuters, March 17, 2022. https://www.reuters.com/article/factcheck-putin-address /fact-check-doctored-video-appears-to-show-putin-announcing-peace -idUSL2N2VK1CC.

Jane Wakefield, "Deepfake Presidents Used in Russia-Ukraine War," *BBC News,* March 18, 2022, https://www.bbc.com/news/technology-60780142.

Gerrit DeVynck, Pranshu Verma, and Jonathan Baran, "Exploding 'Kamikaze' Drones Ushering in New Era of Warfare in Ukraine," *Washington Post,* March 24, 2022, https:// www.washingtonpost.com/technology/2022/03/24/loitering-drone-ukraine/.

Anthony Capaccio, "U.S. Drones for Ukraine Will Include Latest Tank Killers," *Bloomberg. com,* April 4, 2022, https://www.bloomberg.com/news/articles/2022-04-04/u-s -switchblade-drones-for-ukraine-will-include-tank-killers.

Vasco Cotovio and Frederick Pleitgen, "These Drone Operators Used to Make 'Nice' Youtube Videos; Now They Record Alleged Russian War Crimes," *CNN.com,* April 6, 2022, https://www.cnn.com/2022/04/06/europe/ukraine-drone-operators-alleged -russian-crimes-intl/index.html.

Strat watched the race from a helicopter overhead. He says the negative publicity from media outlets about the vehicles failing to reach the finish line ignored the technological achievement of the participants, many of whom were engineering undergraduates or DIY hobbyists. Despite the unrealistic vision of DARPA's planners, 7.4 miles was a new record for a fully autonomous vehicle without a driver at the wheel as backup. The Wright brothers' flight lasted less than 30 seconds, and it was hailed as a remarkable achievement, Strat points out. "This race will be remembered as a monumental event. Don't dismiss this. It was a huge advance."

At the awards banquet in Las Vegas after the race, DARPA director Tether doubled down by announcing a $2 million prize for a second DARPA Grand Challenge in 2005. This time, automakers and tech firms, which had been lurking in the background during the first event, decided to participate with university teams, Strat says, by donating parts and expertise. Stanford partnered with Volkswagen Electronics Research Laboratory; UCLA had help from Intel and Israeli startup MobilEye (purchased by Intel in 2017 for $15 billion); and the University of Florida was sponsored by Smiths Aerospace (now GE Aviation Systems).

The event kicked off in October 2005 on remote roads outside Las Vegas. "The second challenge demonstrated that self-driving vehicles were possible," Strat says. "We wanted vehicles to observe the rules of the road, to follow a driver's handbook, and do everything that drivers need to do to pass an exam with other traffic on the road."

The second challenge was a success, with only one vehicle falling short of the 7.4-mile mark set by the best-performing 2004 entry. Of the 23 vehicles that started the challenge in 2005, five finished the course, including the winner from Stanford, netting the team a $2 million prize. Team leader Sebastian Thrun, then a professor of computer science at Stanford, went on to found both Google X, the corporation's research division and, Google's self-driving division, now known as Waymo. Thrun left Google and is now CEO of the online education firm Udacity and the Kitty Hawk Corporation, which is building electric-powered airplanes. The race set a new standard for technology, automation, and artificial intelligence on the road because it proved that self-driving vehicles could work. Deep-pocketed carmakers understood that an autonomous vehicle that could see its way around obstacles and keep a driver safe had moved into the realm of engineering possibility and began to invest in smaller AI firms that were developing the components of these vehicles.

"The people who built the Grand Challenge vehicles, they all got jobs as leaders at Google, Apple, Tesla, and General Motors," Strat says. These early DARPA events were a kind of graduate school for today's luminaries in the evolving self-driving vehicle industry. In the decade after the 2005 DARPA Grand Challenge, money began flowing from Detroit to Silicon Valley in a race to put autonomous vehicles on the road.

Chris Urmson had cut his teeth at the DARPA Grand Challenge contests. In 2004, he led the Carnegie Mellon team that built Sandstorm. In 2005, his group modified a civilian Hummer H1 called H1ghlander that placed second. CMU also won the 2007 Urban Challenge held at an abandoned military base with a Chevy Tahoe dubbed Boss. After Urmson's successes with designing experimental vehicles, Google hired him in 2009 to direct the tech giant's self-driving car project and build its autonomy software algorithm. He stayed until 2016, when he left to start his own company called Aurora, which bought Uber's failed self-driving unit in December 2020—and went public in the summer of 2021 with an $11 billion valuation.[19]

Today, Urmson leads more than 400 employees at Aurora's headquarters in Pittsburgh and several other locations where the company is building a self-driving platform called the Aurora Driver. It combines AI software, hardware, and data services to completely operate any passenger or commercial vehicle independent of a human driver. The Aurora Driver platform is being tested first in cargo trucks traveling between warehouses in Texas. It's expected to go live in 2022, according to Urmson. "This is really important technology that we're building," he says. "It has the opportunity to make the road safer, to make transportation more efficient, more accessible, more equitable, and less expensive. But to realize these goals, we need to deliver a product where people can have confidence that they're not going to be unreasonably at risk in riding in or having their goods shipped by one of these vehicles."[20] There's a shortage of 60,000 truck drivers in the United States today, a figure that will grow to 160,000 by the end of the decade. Building an autonomous truck will fill that need and make more economic sense than building a robo-taxi. "The value of driving a truckload of goods is many times the value of driving a person," he adds.

Urmson emphasizes that ensuring safety is more than just testing sensors and AI algorithms. It's a way of looking at the entire vehicle-to-human interface and anticipating their interactions. "Safety is not just a function of a bit of software somewhere in the system or a bit of hardware or even the integration of the software to the hardware. It's the process you use to develop it. Are you being thoughtful about making sure that you're only putting it into use in places where it was designed to operate? When something unexpected or bad happens, are you using that [knowledge] to improve and actually make the system safer?"

The Aurora Driver platform uses a combination of cameras, radar, and special long- and medium-range LIDAR (light detection and ranging) that was developed in-house. Aurora is moving step by step, trying to avoid some of the errors that have plagued Tesla's self-driving cars. In 2021, its autonomous trucks began hauling containers of snack foods along a route in Texas between Dallas and Houston. For now, the vehicles always have two safety drivers aboard to take over in construction zones or when cars nearby have turned on emergency blinkers, for example. In the future, Urmson expects the vehicles to be fully autonomous without drivers. In the fall of 2021, Aurora began to carry freight for FedEx between Dallas and Houston along Interstate 45, and the company announced that it plans to expand routes to San Antonio, Las Vegas, and eventually the entire country.[21]

Urmson expects that when autonomous vehicles do take the road alongside vehicles with human drivers, there probably will be accidents. The difference is that the autonomous drivers will be relying on a trail of data rather than shaky human memories of what led to a crash. "Ultimately, something bad is going to happen," Urmson says. "We're going to be building a safe system, but it will fail at some point in ways that we didn't anticipate. It'll also be on the road with other people who are fallible as well."

Urmson says the new fleet of AI-powered trucks will be equipped with devices that record the events before any mishap or accident, much like an aircraft's black box. "We'll be able to look at the data from the vehicle and see what happened. That will allow us to improve the driving for all the vehicles, and understand what the cause of the accident was."

FULLY AUTONOMOUS

Looking back at the past five years, it's apparent that almost every major motor vehicle manufacturer and high-tech company—Tesla, Ford, GM, Aurora, Google's Waymo among others—predicted widespread deployment of automated driving systems by 2020, leading to the disappearance of the human driver.[22] But to date, only a handful of advanced vehicles have been driven on public roads without safety drivers. In addition, as of late 2021, Tesla has been the target of federal safety investigations probing nearly a dozen crashes throughout the United States involving its driver-assist car mode, known as Autopilot.[23] The feature allows drivers to take their hands off the wheel even when changing lanes and navigating through traffic. Some drivers have used Autopilot to text friends, watch Netflix, or even take a nap while driving.[24] That's when the accidents happen. The 2021 probe by the National Highway Traffic Safety Administration probe covers 765,000 Tesla cars.[25]

In February 2022, the NHTSA opened an investigation into more than 350 driver reports of phantom braking of the Tesla while using its advanced driver-assist system, the *Washington Post* reported.[26] Tesla's Autopilot uses cameras, radar, and ultrasonic sensors to support two major features: Traffic-Aware Cruise Control and Autosteer. A similar General Motors system called Super Cruise monitors the driver's eyes and switches off if the person looks away from the road for more than a few seconds. It operates only on major highways.[27]

As a result of Tesla's problems with Autopilot and a 2018 fatal crash involving Uber's self-driving taxi in Phoenix,[28] some firms have pulled back on their expectations. Others are developing limited-use autonomous vehicles that can drive only on specific routes such as interstate highways that are well mapped and well understood by the car's sensors and computer. Even with such limitations, some experts believe it will be many years before a human passenger is driven by a fully autonomous vehicle. Right now, self-driving technology has developed to a hybrid state in which the car performs some functions and drivers can always take over. But humans are easily lulled into a false sense of complacency, says Missy Cummings, a professor of electrical and computer engineering at Duke University, director of the Humans and Autonomy Laboratory and Duke Robotics, and the safety adviser to the National Highway Transportation Safety Board.[29] "The instant that humans start to think that automation performs good enough, they check out mentally."

Cummings studies the relationship between humans and robots as they work together to pilot machines. As one of the US Navy's first female fighter pilots in the 1990s, she saw fatal accidents that were blamed on pilot error and became interested in automated systems and why they couldn't make flying safer. After leaving the military to earn a doctorate in systems engineering at the University of Virginia, she became a faculty member at the Massachusetts Institute of Technology. At Duke, she now works on developing safer systems for autonomous vehicles as well as addressing the legal and social issues linked to autonomy. In the past few years, she's been on a bit of a crusade against Tesla's Autopilot system, arguing both in scientific publications and on Twitter that the human brain is just not ready to allow a car to operate in the current self-driving mode that Tesla has produced. Her concerns were bolstered by her own research and a 2021 study by a team of researchers at MIT, which found that Tesla's Full Self-Driving (FSD) System may not be safe; the team found that drivers may become inattentive when using partially automated driving systems.[30]

The authors followed several hundred Tesla Model S and X owners throughout the greater Boston area. The vehicles were equipped with the cameras and sensors that collect information from the vehicle, record the driver's interaction with the controls, and monitor the driver's posture and eye movements. For the study, MIT collected nearly 500,000 miles' worth of driving data. "Visual behavior patterns change before and after [Autopilot] disengagement," the study's authors wrote. "Before disengagement, drivers looked less on road and focused more on non-driving related areas compared to after the transition to manual driving. The higher proportion of off-road glances before disengagement to manual driving were not compensated by longer glances ahead."

In other words, the study found that drivers stopped looking at the road ahead when Autopilot was engaged, even though Tesla states on its website that its cars "require active driver supervision and do not make the vehicle autonomous." Still, Tesla is using its customers as sort of battery-powered guinea pigs who are collecting data about how well its autonomous system works. Tesla's website also includes a caveat: "With the FSD computer, we expect to achieve a new level of autonomy as we gain billions of miles of experience using our features. The activation and use of these features are dependent on achieving reliability far in excess of human drivers, as well as regulatory approval, which may take longer in some jurisdictions."[31]

Cummings is skeptical about this new level of autonomy and says that it's not just Tesla that must be concerned about the effects of automation on human drivers—other companies have jumped on the autonomous bandwagon, too. For instance, Vay, a German start-up, promises to operate tele-operated self-driving taxis—vehicles that are driven by a human who is elsewhere just as drone aircraft are piloted remotely—in Europe in 2022.[32] The idea is for the customer to drive a car somewhere, then have the vehicle drive itself back to its point of origin. "Tesla has taken it in the shorts quite a bit for Autopilot," Cummings says. "But I think other manufacturers are going to face similar problems soon because . . . the bottom line is that people equate 'hands-free' with 'mind free'—and unfortunately, it's the exact opposite."

Chuck Thorpe's car has blind-spot detection and departure-lane sensors that he helped develop back in the 1990s as part of Navlab. Looking to the future, he says he'd like to see more slow-moving autonomous vehicles on the roads, including a robotic street-sweeper for example. First of all, we would have much cleaner streets. But more importantly, using a low-impact vehicle would build up millions of hours of operation in all kinds of weather to see what works well. From there, other automated possibilities may include mail delivery and garbage pickup. "You want the experience base of what mischievous 12-year-olds are going to do with these automated vehicles—and how . . .to protect yourself," Thorpe says. "Better to learn from a self-driving street-sweeper than a self-driving luxury vehicle," he adds. "You work your way up, rather than starting out with a car going sixty-five miles per hour."

For Thomas Strat, the former DARPA project manager who now runs a firm developing drone aircraft for the Pentagon, the lure of hands-free driving is sometimes too much to resist. When he drives his Tesla from his home in Northern Virginia to work, he finds it most useful in stop-and-go traffic. And sometimes he plays a game with himself. "I close my eyes and see how long I can keep my eyes closed before I can't stand it anymore," Strat says. "My record is three seconds. I know too much about the technology to keep them closed for longer than that. Someday, it will be safe enough."

The journey to a self-driving car began decades ago. Today, it's closer than ever—you may even see one if you live in Boston, San Francisco, or Phoenix. Cars are central to our lives; making them safer and more convenient to operate sparks the imagination of drivers as well as engineers, for whom the notion of a safe and reliable autonomous car presents a problem to solve.

MAKING CITIES SAFER FOR CARS

At MIT's Institute for Data, Systems, and Society, assistant professor Kathy Wu is modeling what happens when autonomous cars and human-driven cars share the same roadways. She wants to know what kind of behaviors might happen, and whether cars can be smart enough to meet the needs of cities, rather than the other way around. In fact, she's found that automated cars might be able to slow traffic jams on freeways and reduce congestion at four-way intersections. This works by having reinforcement learning agents, rather than the individual driver, optimize the speed of the entire traffic flow. "What we found numerically in experiments is that just a very small fraction of vehicles—five to ten percent—can have really outsized impacts on the system," Wu told the Robot Brains Podcast in February 2022.[33] "Five percent of autonomous vehicles can basically eliminate traffic congestion in these model highway settings in a way that we didn't realize was possible."

Reinforcement learning captures the idea behind trial and

error. When it's given an objective, a learning agent attempts to achieve the objective over and over, failing and learning from its mistakes in the process. It was used by AlphaGo, DeepMind's human-beating Go program, for example. Wu's research with reinforcement learning found that adding self-driving cars to a simulated traffic flow can also potentially aid emergency medical vehicles in reaching their destination. "We can model self-driving cars as this helpful agent for the benefit of the system," Wu says.

The same reinforcement-learning techniques can also be applied to lower emissions of planet-warming greenhouse gases by reducing congestion and idling. During simulated studies of grid roads, bottlenecks, and on- and off-ramps, Wu and her colleagues have found that reinforcement learning can match, and in some cases exceed, the performance of current traffic control strategies.[34]

The next step, Wu says, is designing a smartphone app that could help individual drivers make decisions about how to reduce congestion and pollution, allowing humans to behave more like the automated AI-driver. "Instead of just running a regular GPS that tells us which turn to take," Wu says, "it might say speed up a little bit or slow down a little bit."

From early visions for self-driving (and flying) passenger vehicles that many of us read about in comics or saw in TV shows and films, we've now reached a commercial proof of concept stage for these cars (and transport trucks). As with so much that artificial intelligence propels, scaling these efforts will come down to the programmers' and manufacturers' abilities to iron out potentially dangerous system failures—and bolster our trust to a point that we can truly let go. But while Tesla and other companies push the boundaries of self-driving vehicles, some researchers believe that a higher calling for artificial intelligence is to make life better for society as a whole rather than just drivers.

CHAPTER 5

AI's Futurescape

THE TECHNICAL AND PHYSICAL COMPONENTS of artificial intelligence undergo continuous evolution as they enhance products and machines across a spectrum of applications. All of this is happening at lightning speed. By the time you read this book, a few of the innovations described may have been eclipsed by newer or more powerful ones. And entirely new inventions and uses of AI may be introduced, not to mention what will be discovered and created in leading research labs. Building on successes and responding to errors, AI becomes ever more efficient and effective.

In my four decades of involvement in the field I've learned that, as Yogi Berra said, "It's tough to make predictions, especially about the future." Still, there are some things that we do know. One is that scientists, engineers, and data researchers around the globe are deploying AI rapidly and often without considering some of the conflicts about bias, equity, and privacy that have accompanied its use in social media, policing, and employment.

In the early days of AI, expert knowledge was considered the most important feature for the design of AI systems. Today, the use of large volumes of data has become equally or even more important and we're moving toward an era where "data is power." Countries that have the ability and mindset to collect the needed data while suppressing privacy or other civil rights may gain unfair advantages in designing more robust and powerful AI systems. This may cause unexpected developments in health, security, and defense applications.

In this chapter, we'll hear from researchers who are using AI's pattern-detecting powers to sift through information that can help them understand how Earth and our galaxy work. We'll also take a look at a potentially transformative new effort to detect and monitor early signs of dementia and other neurological ailments through the use of "trustworthy" AI, which is the concept that physicians, medical technicians, and patients should be able to understand how the AI agent is making its decisions, and not only whether the resulting diagnosis or answer is accurate. It endeavors to look into the black box that sometimes obscures how AI works. This hope-filled area of research will pair AI scientists like me with physicians, caregivers, and family members to make sure that the data collected by AI-driven sensors are accurate and kept private. At the same time, we want the number-crunching algorithms to be transparent about how they arrive at the decisions they make, especially about possible treatments or medications.

This new "collaboratory"—a collaboration of laboratories—on eldercare and dementia treatment is in its infancy, but its possibilities for pivotal changes in diagnoses, and therefore treatments, are promising and exciting.

Because of these and other evolving applications, I believe that the future is bright for artificial intelligence. But if it's to remain so, understanding data privacy and transparency in decision-making will be key to avoiding conflicts and disparities as its use grows.

AI AND DISASTER RELIEF

Pedro Rodriguez grew up in Puerto Rico in a family of engineers, studied electrical engineering in San Juan, and then moved to Maryland to complete his studies at Johns Hopkins University for his master's degree, and the University of Maryland Baltimore County for his doctoral degree. He's spent the past two decades as a researcher at the Johns Hopkins University Applied Physics Laboratory (APL), just south of Baltimore, where he's a senior technical leader for several AI and machine-learning projects. When Puerto Rico was rocked by the back-to-back disasters of Hurricane Maria in 2017 and a series of powerful earthquakes in late 2019 and 2020, he used what he'd learned to help both his family and his homeland in gratitude for the nourishing years he spent there. Rodriguez has created an AI-based program known as Humanitarian

Assistance for Disaster Relief (HADR) that allows disaster recovery teams to assess in hours what had previously taken days or sometimes weeks. The program finds and marks areas of flooding, blocked roads, and damaged buildings using tools of pattern recognition and deep learning.

"Experiencing hurricanes—knowing especially what my family went through most recently—has played a huge role in my enthusiasm for this project," Rodriguez said in an interview with the APL newsletter.[1] "Once we started using this technology for disaster relief applications, I just knew [it] was an area we could profoundly impact."

Rodriguez and his colleagues at the APL have also devised several algorithm tools based on deep learning to better understand climate change and its impacts on the planet. One program is learning how to predict the formation of Arctic sea ice seven days in advance. Forecasting sea ice has become more difficult to understand as the Arctic polar region warms three times as fast as the rest of the planet. As the Arctic—both its coastlines and open waters—experiences warmer temperatures, accurate forecasts regarding sea ice will become more important for commercial shipping, Alaskan fishing crews, and Indigenous groups in the Alaskan and Canadian Arctic who use it to access hunting and fishing grounds, as well as a transportation route.[2]

In the past, sea ice forecasts were made manually, using satellite data and physics equations to describe the expected expansion or retreat of ice. These equations used meteorological conditions combined with models that take into account how temperature, wind, and the atmosphere influence how sea ice will ebb and flow. "That has been adequate given the amount of activity in the Arctic; they only maybe had to make forecasts for a few ships or for special missions," the APL's Christine Piatko told *Wired* in 2021. "But as there's increased [ship] activity, you can imagine different scenarios where they might need information in a timelier manner. We're trying to anticipate that need." These sea ice forecasts are just one application of artificial intelligence scientists are employing to understand global warming—and how to slow it down. A separate but related experimental effort in Rodriguez's group (now in the proof of concept stage) uses artificial intelligence to estimate greenhouse gas emissions using satellite images of land use, buildings, roads, and forest cover. AI has already done the same thing for small airborne particulates that can cause respiratory health ailments in children and the elderly.[3]

The APL's efforts to deploy AI for climate responses are in good company. In 2019, a group of 22 renowned computer scientists organized by David Rolnick, now assistant professor of computer science at McGill University, came up with a list of uses for AI to combat climate change, from AI-based algorithms that can be used to forecast electric power supply and demand to AI-supported predictions of carbon dioxide emissions of individual power plants or entire nations. The combination of AI and satellite remote sensing can automate detection of methane leaks faster and more efficiently than a human environmental monitor. Plugging these leaks from natural gas wells and pipelines is important because methane is 25 times more powerful than carbon dioxide at trapping heat in the atmosphere. Over the past two centuries, methane concentrations in the atmosphere have more than doubled, due largely to human-related activities. "Because methane is both a powerful greenhouse gas and short-lived compared to carbon dioxide, achieving significant reductions would have a rapid and significant effect on atmospheric warming potential," the US Environmental Protection Agency reported.[4]

AI can also be used to predict improvements in the energy efficiency of office buildings and homes, design more efficient transportation routes for delivery vehicles, and manage electric vehicle battery charging, among other things, according to the paper *Tackling Climate Change with Machine Learning*, presented in 2019 at the world's leading AI conference, NeurIPS (for Neural Information Processing Systems).[5] The paper's many authors—which included academic stars from Stanford and Harvard as well as AI experts at Google, Microsoft, and DeepMind—reminded readers that AI won't cure our ailing planet:

> We emphasize that machine learning is not a silver bullet. The applications we highlight are impactful, but no one

solution will "fix" climate change. . . . Furthermore, technology alone is not enough—technologies that would address climate change have been available for years, but have largely not been adopted at scale by society. While we hope that [machine learning] will be useful in reducing the costs associated with climate action, humanity also must decide to act.

Rodriguez's APL deep-learning program HADR is an example of the kind of action the authors of that paper were hoping to see. It makes damage assessments in a few hours rather than in the days or weeks that previously delayed relief efforts. The program locates and marks areas of flooding, identifies blocked and open roads, and assesses whether buildings are damaged or usable on a four-level scale. In partnership with the Department of Defense's Joint Artificial Intelligence Center, HADR helped recovery efforts after Hurricane Florence and Hurricane Dorian devastated parts of the United States and the Caribbean islands in 2018 and 2019, respectively, and in 2020 after Hurricane Laura, a deadly and destructive Category 4 storm, battered Louisiana.

Rodriguez says it was a coincidence that his disaster assessment algorithm dovetailed with helping people in Puerto Rico cope with several real-world disasters. After Hurricane Maria in 2017, federal officials used HADR to better dispatch aid to hard-hit residents of the island. And in 2020, the same algorithm helped better assess the damage from a magnitude 6.4 earthquake and its aftershocks, which lasted for months and damaged more than eight thousand homes, including some in Rodriguez's Caribbean Sea hometown of Guánica, which was devastated, according to the *New York Times*.[6]

Rodriguez visited Puerto Rico after the initial temblor, and he experienced the aftershocks and tremors the locals understood could go on for a year or more. His family's home was intact, but "the randomness of destruction was shocking," he said in a 2021 interview with the APL. "It was weird to see one house completely destroyed but the house next to it perfectly fine. That just did not compute in my mind. What is the difference between this house and that house?"[7]

Rodriguez envisions a time when artificial intelligence is automatically applied to all kinds of sensor modalities, enabling emergency personnel to respond faster than ever. "I want a future where the sensors looking at the world were designed for AI, instead of sensors designed for human decision-making," Rodriguez says. "In that world, we could respond faster because we wouldn't even need a human in the loop. The AI could simply report 'flooding in this road' and recovery teams could just go, without a need for human confirmation."

SCANNING EARTH

Whether the algorithm is designed to check for homes damaged from an earthquake or to assess infrastructure after a hurricane, one of the easiest, fastest, and most effective jobs for artificial intelligence is monitoring our planet by reviewing images for changes over time. That could mean anything from looking out for illegal deforestation in tropical zones that are important for moderating CO_2 levels and producing oxygen, to stopping illegal fishing in endangered marine habitats. Eric Rignot, a professor of earth system science at the University of California, Irvine, and a senior scientist at NASA's Jet Propulsion Laboratory (JPL) in Pasadena, California, says that AI is already serving as an early warning system for climate change events across the planet. In his lab, machine-learning programs are saving him time, leaving him free to conduct more scientific research. "I don't want to sit at my computer all day looking for icebergs," says Rignot,[8] who was a graduate student of mine while I was at USC. In the early 1990s, Eric and I published several papers on segmenting ice regions from remotely sensed radar images of various types. Little did I know then how important looking at icebergs would be.

As in life, nothing is perfect. And Rignot and Rodriguez agree that the biggest bottleneck in AI's progress in science, medicine, and engineering is not the quality or power of the algorithms, but the pipeline of data from the sensor—whether a high-resolution camera, temperature buoy, or infrared satellite beam—to the researcher. That will require many more independent robotic vehicles that can fly, swim, and crawl through the world to collect information. Today, there are still a lot of humans in the data loop. "Someone has to fly the plane, someone has to save the data on board, bring it to the ground, find the closest place to plug in, and then upload that data to the cloud," Rodriguez says.[9] "Who cares if AI can do this [calculation] in less than two hours if it takes me three days to get the data?" Removing this roadblock will be one of the next big leaps forward.

SCANNING STARS

Just as artificial intelligence has given scientists a view of how the climate is altering landscapes on Earth, it has also boosted the process of discovery in space. And if there's one person who knows about using artificial intelligence to make sense of big data with AI, it's Alexander S. Szalay. The Hungarian-born cosmologist—a Bloomberg Distinguished Professor of Physics and Astronomy as well as Computer Science at the Johns Hopkins University School of Arts and Sciences and the Whiting School of Engineering—is director of the Institute for Data Intensive Engineering and Science (IDIES). In 2020, he was a co-recipient of the Viktor Ambartsumian Prize for International Science for his work on dark matter and his "contributions to data-driven and statistical cosmology."[10]

Szalay's research center at JHU operates massive computer servers that contain datasets from space and the oceans, and the genetic information from human cells. The center holds images from the Sloan Digital Sky Survey (SDSS), an international astronomical collaboration that began in 2000 and now has records on more than 900 million objects. The survey's telescope sits on a mountaintop at the Apache Point Observatory in Sunspot, New Mexico. The SDSS looks at nearby galaxies that are well understood, as well as those that are far away and getting farther. Szalay says that AI algorithms are helping determine what's out there and where to look. "These nearby galaxies are those we actually largely understood," he says. "But for very distant galaxies and very faint galaxies and very faint stars, we have much less accurate information. By the time they finish the survey, we will know what we should have done. So, the question is how we can use AI techniques to help us in picking the objects that we want to observe. What is the follow-up, and how can we use such an AI algorithm that is learning along the way?"[11]

In addition to the SDSS, the IDIES contains the entire dataset for Gaia, a European Space Agency satellite that's measuring the distances between more than a billion objects in the Milky Way.[12] The institute also hosts the results of a set of high-resolution general circulation models that help physical oceanographers understand the dynamics of the Earth's ocean circulation in the past and present, while providing predictions of the future, as well as high-level data for more than 70,000 published human RNA samples, making it possible for researchers to study gene expression on an unprecedented scale.

Szalay says that with all this information available in computer storage, it's becoming more important to manage that data and make good decisions about what to collect and what to ignore. Making things more difficult is the fact that the hundreds of scientists, educators, and technology developers who use the institute's datasets each have their own specific research agenda. "We're getting good at collecting data, but we're doing it in a dumb way," he explains. "We're collecting lots of data with the premise that we will at some point sort it out. And as a result, 90 percent of the stuff that we collect is probably garbage." Szalay recalls asking colleagues at a research conference whether they have enough data or if they would like more. "Everybody of course screams 'We want more!'" Szalay says. "But what they mean is each of them wants a different kind of data that is relevant for their own personal research, and they don't care about the rest." As science is becoming increasingly complex, it's already surpassed the point where a single human can comprehend all the angles of some of these large experiments like the SDSS or human genetics. Szalay believes that AI can help slow down the firehose of information that is filling data servers round the planet, or at least make better decisions about what kind of data will be more relevant to answering scientific questions and solving societal problems. "We're getting to the point when we trust our AI to drive our cars," he adds. "Why can't [AI] drive our telescopes or genomic sequences, or any other instrument in science?"

TRUSTING AI'S DECISIONS

Szalay, Rodriguez, and others who study the physical world
through the lens of enormous digital datasets rely on the tools
of artificial intelligence not only to collect that information
but also to make decisions about which points to collect, how
they should be stored, and even what kind of questions scientist should ask it. But when it comes to AI and people, we're
not quite there yet. Reliable, safe, and trustworthy AI systems
and tools are essential as artificial intelligence moves into
medicine. As populations grow older, AI may have a unique
role to play in managing the problems of an aging society.
Among other capabilities, it can take the guesswork out of the
dosage and choice of medications, almost like having a personal physician assistant in a virtual form.

Americans are living longer. The median lifespan of girls
born in 2010 is almost 86 years, up from 80.3 years born in
1960; for boys, it's 82 years, up from 74.8.[13] In addition, cen-
sus-based projections indicate that by 2030, one in five US residents will be age 65 and older.[14] The problem is that although
people are living longer, they're not necessarily healthier,
which poses significant future health care challenges. While
we face many of these issues today, they'll be compounded by
the volume of incidences with the ballooning over-65 population. Problem areas include polypharmacy—taking multiple
medications for multiple diseases, often prescribed by differ-

ent doctors who aren't aware of the patient's other medications—which can cause problematic interactions; forgetting to take medicines; hindered mobility, which leads to falls and frailty; and social isolation. One approach for resolving these problems is designing personalized AI systems. The artificial intelligence agent will only use the data collected by you and used for your medical condition. They're your data. They're not trained on any other patients. That's the goal of personalized medicine powered by AI.

There are other health care challenges in an aging population, including increased prevalence of Alzheimer's disease and related dementias, thereby emphasizing the need for personalized solutions for eldercare. This means that there's a need to develop new assistance and monitoring tools driven by AI that can detect problems, and improve or at least maintain the health and well-being of elderly persons and their caregivers, particularly those who live alone. That's especially true because each person has a unique mix of underlying conditions, diet, and exercise routines, and physical and mental health issues—as well as disease states.

In 2018, the National Academy of Medicine recommended that a patient's personalized health information system track the patient over time, taking into account their overall health, treatment, preventive management, and input gathered from appropriate sources, including the patient, clinician, the laboratory, and other testing. Daily checks of simple vital signs, such as blood pressure, blood sugar, or heart rate, can help people make choices about diet and exercise that prevent or reduce the impacts of big problems in years to come. In 2021, we began addressing the academy's recommendation and formed the Johns Hopkins Artificial Intelligence and Technology Collaboratory for Aging Research, which will combine personalized medicine and health with artificial intelligence. In addition to myself, the center, funded by an NIH grant, is being led by a team that includes Peter Abadir, a geriatrician with extensive research expertise on molecular measurements and biomarkers of physical and cognitive decline in older adults; Gregory Hager, the Mandell Bellmore Professor of Computer Science and the founding director of the Johns Hopkins Malone Center for Engineering in Healthcare; and Jeremy Walston, a geriatrician, the deputy director of the Johns Hopkins Division of Geriatric Medicine and Gerontology, and the principal investigator of the Johns Hopkins Older Americans Independence Center, with expertise in biological and clinical translational frailty and resiliency research.

The new multidisciplinary effort is being developed jointly by faculty across Hopkins's Whiting School of Engineering, the School of Medicine, and the Carey Business School. This national center will ensure that any innovations will be easily accessible to traditionally underserved populations of older adults in both urban and rural areas throughout the United States.

HELPING AT HOME

How will our research on medicine and AI help? Imagine you're elderly. AI sensors could be used to determine your overall frailty: how you walk, complete certain tasks, and speak. This is important because falling is one of the biggest concerns of elderly patients. These sensors can be designed to measure different gait parameters and cadences, data that can be used to diagnose a developing condition that is otherwise difficult to detect, or warn a caregiver of a more immediate problem such as a fall or a stroke. Other kinds of sensors can detect early signs of dementia through slightly altered speech patterns. The big trick is how to get a patient to activate these sensors without restricting movements. The solution may be embedding them in clothing, for example, or a watch, or perhaps mounting a camera sensor that gives the patient and maybe a caregiver a simple warning when things aren't going well. While these gait and speech sensors are a good idea, they're not yet developed to the point where they can be used in clinical practice. Already more generalized sensors are on the market that can tell whether someone has fallen down, for example, but they don't have the predictive capability for neurological conditions that we're hoping to achieve. At the same time, the brains behind these AI-driven sensors must be built so they can be trained to make safe and accurate decisions. This will take time. Many of these solutions will need not only lab testing but also approval by federal regulators before they can be patented and applied for the public's use.

My role as a collaborator will be to develop several tools in an AI suite to monitor the progression of dementia in older patients. Those tools will work together with others to classify patients according to frailty scores (that is, frail, intermediate, or robust) by employing biomechanical mobility, cognitive, and mood evaluations. Given that the severity of frailty and stage of dementia may impact the needed care, we will also develop tools to enhance the ability of caregivers to provide personalized support for elderly individuals. In the longer term, AI will be able to classify and predict, based on longitudinal data, individuals' levels of needed care before they reach a state of frailty; provide classification for frailty trends in a prospective aging cohort; and correctly predict responses to interventions or treatment.

We will have patient volunteers wear devices for measuring gait parameters such as stride and cadence. As part of a three-year DARPA effort from 2000 to 2003, I developed several methods for gait-based human identification at a distance. This work can be adapted and repurposed to estimate gait parameters and monitor changes in them as a person gets older. My group, in collaboration with Thomas P. Andriacchi's group at Stanford University, also developed a system for motion capture using four to eight cameras. Recently, my group developed an approach for 3D modeling of humans from a single image. Many of these technologies can be repurposed, reimagined, and evaluated for clinical translation and validation in the new Johns Hopkins AI center.

Devices that track eye movements as well as algorithms will be critical for evaluating the cognitive state and mood of elderly individuals. Video and image-processing techniques could be used to evaluate facial paralysis and strokes or to recognize emotions. Over the years, I've developed several algorithms for recognizing facial expressions (sad, angry, neutral, happy, anxious, and so on),[15] as well as the small muscle movements, known as "action units" that contribute to facial expressions.[16] A recent paper has discussed the effectiveness of facial expressions determined from online videos in detecting Parkinson's disease.[17] Speech and language-related measurements can also provide useful information to evaluate motor and cognitive impairments, which are common in elderly populations. Collection of all of this personal identifiable information (PII) will need to be bound by strict privacy rules and rigorous institutional review protocols.

My colleague Najim Dehak, an associate professor of electrical and computer engineering at Johns Hopkins, and his group have used machine-learning techniques to detect and assess Parkinson's disease in several cohorts by leveraging the information present in the kinetic aspects of their speech.[18] The group has employed natural-language processing technologies to assess the cognitive state of patients with Alzheimer's disease and to analyze sentiment and emotions.[19]

Another example of emerging sensors is a device built by Origin Wireless, a small business located in College Park, Maryland, that uses wireless AI algorithms to scan indoor environments and the people inside them. The Origin approach significantly improves the resolution of indoor sensing and positioning. It can detect the tiniest of movements, such as the rise and fall of a human chest as the lungs take in air and the heart beats. This kind of contact-free sensor is useful for sleep monitoring; it's also practical for getting precise estimates of the walking speed for indoor tracking—detecting falls as well as monitoring gait and heart rate variability. It's exciting that—by using WiFi ambient radio waves—all this information can be collected without attaching a device to the patient.

One of the challenges of introducing physical and mental health monitoring devices in and around elderly patients is the potential loss of privacy. Embedded cameras or microphones such as Amazon's Alexa or Echo Show can be helpful in evaluating and monitoring various health conditions, for example by connecting to sensors that detect when an elderly person may have fallen and then transmitting an alert to a caregiver. Amazon unveiled this "Alexa Together" service for families in December 2021.[20] The challenge is the security of the data they collect. In our research project, patients (or caregivers) will be given the option of turning off the data collection device at any time. Amazon maintains that their devices are "designed to protect your privacy—Amazon is not in the business of selling your personal information to others,"[21] but some experts have raised concerns that federal regulations don't cover many home medical-monitoring devices and worry that internet-connected devices might pose a risk to individuals' private data.[22]

AI can also help the blind or those with compromised vision. For decades, researchers and the companies to which they sell the technology have built mobility and wayfinding systems like smart canes and accessible routing applications that provide a range of audio or hand-held feedback for people with low vision.[23] While at the University of Maryland, I supervised three groups of honors undergraduate students in a program to build prototypes of outdoor and indoor navigation devices using video cameras and Kinect face-recognition systems. As part of the program, the students and I interacted with experts at the National Federation of the Blind in Baltimore and the Columbia Lighthouse for the Blind in Silver Spring, Maryland. We learned firsthand about the challenges in building interfaces between the sensors and algorithms on the one hand, and the people using them on the other.

AI FOR GOOD

I'm tremendously excited about the new push to combine personalized health care and AI to help elderly patients. It's another example of "AI for Good," a theme that continues to grow throughout our field. At the same time that we strive to help patients, other researchers are anticipating some of the unforeseen aspects of both artificial intelligence and autonomy. Cara LaPointe spent her early career in the US Navy, designing autonomous systems and ships while studying how to integrate the two. At the Woods Hole Oceanographic Institution's Deep Submergence Lab in Falmouth, Massachusetts, she conducted research in underwater robotics, developing sensor fusion algorithms for deep-ocean autonomous underwater vehicle navigation. Today, she is codirector of the Johns Hopkins Institute for Assured Autonomy, a cross-disciplinary effort to understand some of the big conflicts in which people, robots, and AI intersect. These conflicts are already here, according to LaPointe. "If you can't trust it, you're not going to use it," she says. "As we move into a world where there's more and more AI, it's very difficult to know when a system is going to operate safely and when it's going to fail."

LaPointe says that trusting AI isn't important only when we're driving hands-free in a Tesla; it's also vital when it makes decisions about a medical prognosis, detects credit card fraud, or helps to decide who gets hired. "Technology is always created for all the good stuff you can do, but then bad stuff happens—whether it's intentional or unintentional," LaPointe says. "We spend a lot of time thinking about what could go wrong. And how do you prevent that?"[24] For mobile robots to move safely and follow social norms in human spaces, they must anticipate how humans move and interact. When two people are talking in a hospital hallway, for example, a delivery robot can't just walk through them. It's important to consider the impact of a robot's or AI agent's actions on human performance as one of the device's abilities.

LaPointe and her colleagues say their goal at this new center is to develop autonomous agents, robots, and vehicles that move just as comfortably indoors as outside—and that consider both social and physical boundaries as humans. "How do you start to get the robots not just to understand people as objects to be navigated around, but to understand the social dynamics of people so that the robots can behave in more predictable ways?" says LaPointe.

TO TRUST, VERIFY

Looking at the vast universe of artificial intelligence and its applications, and some of the researchers with whom I spoke in writing this book, the way forward is captivating and heartening, if unpredictable. If people are going to trust AI—and the humans like me who create it—there will have to be a new generation of software designers and computer scientists who understand not only the opportunities and limitations of AI, but its ethical issues as well.

Already, European lawmakers have proposed new rules on

AI that could affect how Silicon Valley does business in the European Union. The proposal, which was released in April 2021, bans some uses of AI, heavily regulates high-risk uses, and lightly regulates less risky AI systems, according to a 2021 analysis by the Brookings Institution.[25] Forbidden are AI systems that cause or are likely to cause "physical or psychological harm" through the use of "subliminal techniques" or by exploiting "the vulnerabilities of a specific group of persons due to their age, physical, or mental disability." It prohibits AI systems from providing social scoring for general purposes by public authorities. It also precludes the use of "real-time" remote biometric identification systems for law enforcement purposes, such as facial recognition, in publicly accessible spaces. In the United States, Congress has held several rounds of hearings on AI and bias, and a White House task force on research and innovation in AI is expected to make its first recommendations in 2022.[26] The task force—co-chaired by the White House Office of Science and Technology Policy and the National Science Foundation—will create a blueprint for AI researchers and students across several disciplines; it will also detail requirements for ensuring security, privacy, civil rights, and civil liberties.

Chinese officials aren't waiting to hear from an American task force or for public comment. In February 2022, the government announced restrictions on the commercial use of AI. They prohibit fake accounts, manipulating traffic numbers,

The Four Fearsome Elephants in the Room

Artificial intelligence technology has seen its ups and downs over the decades, the down periods being referred to as "AI winters," when the federal government withdrew funding as confidence in the technology decreased. Since 2012, when the powerful new branch of AI known as deep learning emerged, investors, the public, and the media have contributed to an exuberant narrative about what AI can achieve.

Yet, another AI ice age may arise in the near future if researchers and engineers don't seriously address the issues of bias, data domain shifts, privacy concerns, and vulnerability to adversarial attacks. These destructive beasts in the AI space must be tamed for us to see the adoption of more of AI's contributions to society in everything from agriculture to health care to national security.

Bias: As discussed in chapter 3, facial recognition systems have often performed poorly when identifying darker skinned people. This problem has now morphed into a general AI bias concern across other AI algorithms or systems. My own and several other teams are developing methods for detecting and mitigating bias in facial recognition. This problem also arises in the design of AI systems for medicine and health care: pulse oximeters that measure oxygen levels by beaming light through the skin and then blood, for example, are affected by skin pigmentation.

Data domain shifts: Modern AI systems are being trained using speech, photo, text, and video data that are labeled with tags known as annotations. If we test the AI system on data that's collected by a different microphone or camera than is used in the final product, the performance usually declines. An Alexa trained for a native English speaker will not at first perform well when tested using speech data collected from a non-native English speaker, while a self-driving car trained using data collected in Phoenix, Arizona, may not perform as well in Mumbai, India, where the city plans, roads, obstacles, and laws are so different. Such performance incongruities can cast doubt on the technology and the decisions being made around it, especially in health care applications. In turn, this can slow funding, which ultimately limits the development of solutions. However, these deficiencies can be addressed by adding more training data from the test domain. Assuring performance in the presence of domain shift is something many groups in the world, including ours, are working on, but we're nowhere near developing the solution that will lead to a high-performing, robust system.

Privacy concerns: How data used to train deep learning–based AI is obtained has become a major issue that could slow progress. In fact, privacy concerns have contributed to several US cities and several countries limiting or even banning the use of facial recognition systems by police agencies, many of which use a controversial software program by Clearview AI that is the subject of several lawsuits. To protect individual privacy while still achieving accurate identification of subjects, my group and several other teams are testing whether we can use synthetic data—or facial images generated by computers—in the training set. But many other privacy issues need to be addressed, including how AI systems can hear our conversations, read our emails and other posts, and create a profile that can be exploited for good (recommender systems that consumers willingly opt into) or nefarious purposes.

Vulnerability to cyberattacks: Since 2013, it's become both a hobby and a system test for some researchers to come up with various ways of attacking deep learning–based AI systems in order to check for vulnerabilities. These attacks are known by many names—noise attacks, semantic attacks, FGSM attacks, PGD attacks, Carlini-Wagner attacks, and patch attacks. We frequently hear or read about malicious attacks (some of which are ransom ploys, while others are aimed at national security or to undermine a corporation's reputation) that cause deep learning–based systems to perform poorly—or not at all for certain periods. While increasingly robust defense systems are being designed to maintain continuity in the presence of these attacks, the performance drop could be significant, raising doubts about the full-scale deployment of AI systems in the near future. These attacks threaten businesses, banks, health care delivery, municipal grids, national security, and many more institutions upon which society depends.

and promoting addictive content, according to a report in *Wired*.[27] Under the rules, companies will be barred from charging customers different prices based on their personal characteristics and will be required to notify users when AI-based algorithms are used to make recommendations. Of course, these new rules may be nearly impossible to enforce, as the behavior of algorithms continually changes as it adapts to new information or data.

THE FUTURE OF AI

In such a dynamic and fast-moving field of study and applications that has seen its share of stops and starts and ups and downs, it's even harder to be prescient, but here are some potential future directions for AI.

In 2003, DARPA announced a program called LifeLog. The objective was to compile a massive electronic database of people's every activity and relationship. This was to include credit card purchases, websites visited, the content of telephone calls and e-mails sent and received, scans of faxes and postal mail sent and received, instant messages sent and received, books and magazines read, television and radio program selections, physical locations, and biomedical data recorded through wearable GPS sensors. The high-level goal of this data logging was to identify "preferences, plans, goals, and other markers of intentionality."[28] Many now feel that smartphones, fitness bracelets, and social media platforms introduced after 2003 could provide similar capabilities. Due to privacy concerns, this program was canceled in 2004 even before contracts were given out.[29]

Now, let's fast-forward to 2022. Given the explosive amounts of information we now have to deal with on a daily basis, it's tempting to imagine an AI assistant that could process the multi-modal data collected by us, for us, and about us and provide useful guidance and advice. Of course, we need to make sure the privacy of the users, as well as those they are interacting with, is strictly protected as well as ensure strong robustness to hacks and adversarial attacks on collected data.

When I came to the United States in 1977, telephone calls to India were so expensive (I couldn't afford to call my parents with a monthly after-tax salary of $267) that the first time I was able to talk to my parents was a good three years after I arrived here—and decades before email or texts. Things got a little better in the mid-1980s, when we could make person-to-person calls (you don't get charged until the person you wish to talk to is available). Many of my friends and relatives have elderly parents in India under the care of siblings (if they're lucky enough to have them living in the same town) or who are somehow able to live by themselves. Having an AI assistant, even for elderly parents a few blocks away, could be quite useful in keeping track of their health and activities. But a balance must be struck between the effectiveness of such devices and privacy concerns, one of the issues that led to the cancellation of the LifeLog program and that remains relevant today. The only advantage is that we do have significantly improved AI capabilities to even think of this possibility and are more cognizant of issues such as privacy and robustness to adversarial attacks.

Another area where I believe AI could be useful is in providing assistance to people with visual or hearing disabilities. Limited user studies have indicated great potential for these technologies to be enhanced using AI tools. The same can be said for future research into developing better AI technologies for sign language, thereby improving the quality of life for people with hearing loss. Themes such as human-centered AI, personalized AI, and privacy-preserving learning, will be central to realizing such AI devices.

AI-based tools and systems will have a huge impact on education. To improve the efficiency of teachers while improving the outcomes of students, AI processes that interact and collaborate both between the teacher and machine, as well as between the machine and student, will lead to personalization of content, allowing instructors to employ knowledge they have of their students to be supplemented with AI-assisted self-assessments.[30]

Finally, AI-based tools will help dispel misinformation that's prevalent in our societies. Many of us are aware of the consequences of deepfakes—in which images or videos are manipulated, often with malicious intent, to mislead viewers—which ironically are enabled by some AI tools. Some of my recent research has been focused on detecting and countering these, just as we do for computer-based cyberattacks.

Recent developments arising out of DARPA projects such as MediFor, SemaFor, and GARD point to progress that is being made using AI-based tools to mitigate the bad effects resulting from falsification of information.[31] I believe AI-based tools and apps can ultimately be programmed to be our watchguards and protect our way of life.

Beyond its continued research funding, artificial intelligence's future growth is dependent on addressing four core issues: bias when applied to people and social systems; further refinements in its abilities to adapt to different kinds of data, environments, sensors, cultures and societies; privacy; and weaponizing applications of its technologies, including deepfake attacks and other rogue uses.

AI is integrated into our laboratories, leisure activities, homes, hospitals, public spaces, schools, vehicles, and workplaces. So—*can* we trust it? In thousands of instances, yes, and more so as engineers and programmers work to resolve its endemic problems.

But even if we bulletproof every application of the technologies to ensure that they're perfectly equitable, ethical, and safe, one enduring problem will always remain: Artificial intelligence, in the hands of people with nefarious intent, can and will be misused despite the best intentions of its creators.

This is not specific to AI—many other technologies including nuclear, biological, and chemical have positive uses but are maliciously manipulated by people and nations. AI must be regulated as those technologies are so that only applications that enhance and protect our lives are encouraged and sustained. There are no AI regulatory commissions at national or international levels that establish rules and regulations (although in 2021, the European Commission proposed the first global regulatory attempt, The Artifical Intelligence Act, which has not yet been enacted); perhaps that time has come. The balance between benefits and risks must be struck.

The thrill of ever-expanding applications of these innovations drives our expectations of what AI could—or should—do next, ever upping the ante, which is further fueled by science fiction dreams of what's possible. Research has many miles to go to approach the loftiest of these visions; we need to exercise patience as kinks are worked out, problems are resolved, and teams now working have the chance to build the next generations of devices and solutions. The process of reaching brings ancillary benefits. As mentioned in chapter 4, for instance, while fully autonomous cars may not be available yet, the goal of building them has introduced safety features that are already saving lives. For science to move forward, the demand for perfection can't undermine the quests.

Acknowledgments

THROUGHOUT MY FOUR-DECADE CAREER, I've encountered numerous individuals who, knowingly or not, have strongly influenced my development, both academically and personally. I've been extremely fortunate to have received 360-degree mentoring from some of the pioneers in the fields of computer vision, pattern recognition, and artificial intelligence, along with colleagues in many universities and companies, and professors and fellow students in my graduate and undergraduate classes. Alas, there is not enough space to individually mention and thank all those who have mentored me.

My parents, Muthukrishnan Ramalingam and Ramalingam Kamakshi, inspired me and encouraged me to pursue an academic career.

M. A. L. Thathachar, who taught my first graduate course on pattern recognition at the Indian Institute of Science (IISc), and my master's thesis adviser, E. V. Krishnamurthy at IISc, instilled in me a passion for academic research. My career was shaped at Purdue University by brilliant scholars including my doctoral adviser R. L. Kashyap, King-Sun Fu, and Keinosuke Fukunaga. During my graduate studies at Purdue, I also had the privilege of studying under Azriel Rosenfeld, a groundbreaking computer vision scientist at the University of

Maryland. In addition, I had the opportunity to interact with Jack Sklansky at the University of California, Irvine, and a bit later with Thomas S. Huang, leading researchers in pattern recognition and computer vision, respectively. I owe a great deal to all of these outstanding researchers for settling me on a wonderful academic journey, and I'm grateful to them for inspiring me and mentoring me over the years. Azriel and I became colleagues when I moved to the University of Maryland in 1991. Given the amount of time I spent with him, first as a student and then as a colleague, it's not an exaggeration to say that he is singularly responsible for who I am and where I am today. I am profoundly grateful to him.

My years as an academic have taken me to three universities: the University of Southern California, the University of Maryland, and, since August 2020, Johns Hopkins University. I had, and have, the privilege of interacting with the world's best minds not only in my core areas of interest, but also in related areas such as signal processing, communications, and information and controls theory. I'd like to particularly thank Alexander A. Sawchuk, Larry S. Davis, and K. J. Ray Liu for their collegiality and friendship. I've also enjoyed collaborations with many colleagues in industries and government laboratories. Specifically, I'd like to thank Thomas Strat at DZYNE Technologies and Jonathon Phillips at the National Institute of Standards and Technology.

While professors teach students, they soon realize that the students also teach them in return. A successful professor is one who learns from his students. I have had the pleasure of supervising 115 doctoral dissertations, 23 masters' theses, and 14 postdoctoral fellowships. My students have taught me much more than they may acknowledge or even be aware of. Every one of them is accomplished in their chosen careers in universities including Arizona State University, Carnegie Mellon University, Iowa State, the Indian Institute of Science, the Indian Institutes of Technology, Johns Hopkins University, Purdue University, Rice University, the University of California, Riverside, and the University of California, Santa Barbara. Many work in industries and government laboratories, including Amazon, Apple, Facebook, Google, and the US Army Research Laboratory. I continue to learn from my current students. All the successes I've had in my career are due to placing myself between brilliant teachers and gifted students.

Although I've been at Johns Hopkins University for less than two years, I'm already involved in several productive research collaborations and am looking forward to more such interactions. The Hopkins ecosystem is tuned to interdisciplinary research in every direction, and I intend to make use of the opportunities afforded here. I'd like to thank Denis Wirtz, vice provost of research, and Julie Messersmith, executive director for research in Hopkins's Office of Research, for their support of the Bloomberg Distinguished Professors program as well as Barbara Kline Pope, executive director and publisher of Johns Hopkins University Press, for involving me in the Wavelengths program.

This book would not have been possible without the patience and intellect of Eric Niiler, who was instrumental in shaping, researching, and writing this book; the vision and guidance of Wavelengths program director Anna Marlis Burgard; and the keen editing skills of Charles Dibble at Johns Hopkins University Press. My thanks go to all of you.

Finally, I would like to thank my dear wife, Vishnu Priya, and our children, Vivek and Deepa. I am grateful beyond measure for your love and support.

Glossary

Here are some common terms that describe the components and functions of AI software programs as they begin to think and learn more like humans.

algorithm. A digital, mathematical set of instructions that enables processes or solves a class of problems. Algorithms can perform calculation, data processing, and automated reasoning tasks.

application programming interface (API). A bit of programming that allows elements of software or computers to communicate with each other. Every time you use an app, send an instant message, or check the weather on your phone, you're engaging an API.

artificial intelligence (AI). The science of creating machines and/or technology that can reason, learn, plan, and make predictions—tasks normally requiring human intelligence—that may in fact surpass human capabilities.

artificial neural network (ANN). A mathematical model that receives inputs such as speech, image, or video and generates outputs including a word or identity of an object(s) in an image. Neural networks rely on enormous troves of reference training data to learn and improve their accuracy over time. However, once these learning algorithms are fine-tuned for accuracy, they're powerful tools in computer science and artificial intelligence, allowing us to classify and cluster data at a high velocity. One of the most well-known neural networks is Google's search algorithm.

computer vision. The capability of a computer system to interpret data in a manner that is similar to the way humans use their senses to relate to the world around them.

deepfake. An image that has been manipulated with malicious intent using the tools of deep learning.

deep learning (DL). An area of machine learning that attempts to mimic the activity in layers of neurons in the human brain to learn how to recognize complex patterns in data. The "deep" in deep learning refers to the large number of layers of neurons that help to learn rich representations of data to achieve better performance gains.

machine learning (ML). A computer's ability to learn a specific task, using algorithms and data, without being explicitly programmed to do so, relying instead on patterns and inference.

natural language processing (NLP). A subfield of computer science, information engineering, and artificial intelligence centered on giving computers the ability to turn human speech into written text or to translate it into other languages.

pattern recognition. The automated discovery of patterns in data through the use of computer algorithms to take actions such as classifying that data into different categories.

Sources: Stuart J. Russell and Peter Norvig, *Artificial Intelligence: A Modern Approach,* 4th ed. (Boston: Pearson, 2022); IBM Cloud Education; Wikipedia.

Notes

PREFACE

1. Mark Tran, "Deep Blue Computer Beats World Chess Champion" [archive, 1996], *The Guardian*, February 12, 2021, https://www.theguardian.com /sport/2021/feb/12/deep-blue-computer-beats-kasparov-chess-1996.

2. Christine Fritsch, "Why the Government Market for Artificial Intelligence Technology Is Expanding," *Federal Times*, September 28, 2021, https:// www.federaltimes.com/thought-leadership/2021/09/28/why-the -government-market-for-artificial-intelligence-technology-is-expanding/.

3. PR Newswire, "Global Artificial Intelligence (AI) Market to Reach $228.3 Billion by 2026," May 18, 2021, https://www.prnewswire.com /news-releases/global-artificial-intelligence-ai-market-to-reach-228-3 -billion-by-2026–301293951.html.

4. "Best Undergraduate Artificial Intelligence Programs," *U.S. News & World Report*, https://www.usnews.com/best-colleges/rankings/computer-science /artificial-intelligence.

CHAPTER 1. THE BIRTH AND GROWTH OF AI

1. Gary Marcus and Ernest Davis, *Rebooting AI: Building Artificial Intelligence We Can Trust* (New York: Vintage, 2020), 13.

2. Charles Isbell, dean and professor of computing, Georgia Institute of Technology, and director of the Laboratory for Interactive Artificial Intelligence, in conversation with Eric Niiler, July 8, 2021.

3. Eric Niiler, "The Robot Ships Are Coming . . . Eventually," *Wired*, October 30, 2020, https://www.wired.com/story/mayflower-autonomous-ships/.

4. NASA Science Mars Exploration Program, "AI Is Helping Scientists

Discover Fresh Craters on Mars," October 1, 2020, https://mars.nasa.gov /news/8765/ai-is-helping-scientists-discover-fresh-craters-on-mars/.

5. NASA/California Institute of Technology Jet Propulsion Laboratory, "Robotic Navigation Tech Will Explore the Deep Ocean," May 14, 2021, https://www.jpl .nasa.gov/news/robotic-navigation-tech-will-explore-the-deep-ocean.

6. James Bellingham, executive director, Johns Hopkins University Institute for Assured Autonomy, in conversation with Eric Niiler, January 14, 2022.

7. Ray Stern, "Angry Residents, Abrupt Stops: Waymo Vehicles Are Still Causing Problems in Arizona," *Phoenix New Times,* March 31, 2021, https:// www.phoenixnewtimes.com/news/waymo-arizona-abrupt-stops -angry-residents-are-still-a-problem-11541896.

8. Kathleen McGrory and Neil Bedi, "Targeted," Tampa Bay Times, September 3, 2020, https://projects.tampabay.com/projects/2020 /investigations/police-pasco-sheriff-targeted/intelligence-led-policing/; Associated Press, "Tampa Bay Times Wins 13th Pulitzer for Reporting," June 11, 2021, https://apnews.com/article/fl-state-wire-tampa-arts-and -entertainment-a5c13b8f070ef67ae16f28aac8b81f35.

9. "Federal Judge Rejects Sheriff's Office's Attempt to Dismiss Lawsuit Challenging 'Predictive Policing' Program," *10 Tampa Bay,* August 4, 2021, https://www.wtsp.com/article/news/local/pascocounty/judge-rejects -pasco-county-sheriff-lawsuit-dismissal-predictive-policing-program /67-5015f72a-edc1-46a0-9bdf-5e0885483e75.

10. Vincent Brussee, "China's Social Credit System Is Actually Quite Boring," *Foreign Policy,* September 15, 2021, https://foreignpolicy.com/2021/09/15 /china-social-credit-system-authoritarian/.

11. Grandview Research, "Artificial Intelligence Market Size, Share and Trends Analysis Report" June 2021, report no. GVR-1-68038-955-5, https://www.grandviewresearch.com/industry-analysis/ artificial-intelligence-ai-market.

12. IBM Cloud Education, "Machine Learning," July 15, 2020, https://www.ibm .com/cloud/learn/machine-learning.

13. Marcus and Davis, *Rebooting AI*, 47.

14. Stuart J. Russell and Peter Norvig, *Artificial Intelligence: A Modern Approach*, 3rd ed. (Boston: Pearson, 2016), 30.

15. Vannevar Bush, "As We May Think," *The Atlantic*, July 1945, https://www.theatlantic.com/magazine/archive/1945/07/as-we-may-think/303881/.

16. Jay L. Zagorsky, "Rise and Fall of the Landline," *The Conversation*, March 14, 2019, https://theconversation.com/rise-and-fall-of-the-landline-143-years-of-telephones-becoming-more-accessible-and-smart-113295.

17. Alan Turing, "Computing Machinery and Intelligence," *Mind* 59, no. 126 (October 1950), 433-460, https://doi.org/10.1093/mind/LIX.236.433.

18. Russell and Norvig, *Artificial Intelligence*, 2.

19. Oscar Schwartz, "Why People Demanded Privacy to Confide in the World's First Chatbot," *IEEE Spectrum*, November 18, 2019, https://spectrum.ieee.org/tech-talk/artificial-intelligence/machine-learning/why-people-demanded-privacy-to-confide-in-the-worlds-first-chatbot.

20. Jeff Davis, "How Many Million Lines of Code Does It Take?," *Visual Capitalist*, February 8, 2017, https://www.visualcapitalist.com/millions-lines-of-code/.

21. Marcus and Davis, *Rebooting AI*, 30.

22. Taylor Kubota, "Stanford's Robotics Legacy," *Stanford News*, January 16, 2019, https://news.stanford.edu/2019/01/16/stanfords-robotics-legacy/.

23. William van Melle, "MYCIN: A Knowledge-Based Consultation Program for Infectious Disease Diagnosis," *International Journal of Man-Machine Studies* 10, no. 3 (May 1978): 313-322, https://www.sciencedirect.com/science/article/abs/pii/S0020737378800492.

24. Victor L. Yu, Lawrence M. Fagan, Sharon M. Wraith, et al., "Antimicrobial Selection by a Computer: A Blinded Evaluation by Infectious Disease Experts," *JAMA* 242, no. 12 (1979): 1279-1282, https://doi:10.1001/jama.1979.03300120033020.

25. Russell and Norvig, *Artificial Intelligence*, 24

26. T. R. Reid, "Japanese Government Ends Development of Computer,"

Washington Post, June 2, 1992, https://www.washingtonpost.com/archive/
business/1992/06/02/japanese-government-ends-development-of-computer
/97184ba9-7177-4516-82f9-d684aecd1f24/.

27. IBM Cloud Education, "Neural Networks," August 17, 2020, https://www.
ibm.com/cloud/learn/neural-networks.

28. Alex Krizhevsky, Ilya Sutskever, and Geoffrey E. Hinton, ImageNet
Classification with Deep Convolutional Neural Networks," *Communications
of the ACM* 60 no. 6 (June 2018): 84-90, https://papers.nips.cc/paper/2012
/file/c399862d3b9d6b76c8436e924a68c45b-Paper.pdf.

29. Stefanie T. L. Pöhlmann, Elaine F. Harkness, Christopher J. Taylor, and
Susan M. Astley, "Evaluation of Kinect 3D Sensor for Healthcare Imaging,"
Journal of Medical and Biological Engineering 36, no 6 (2016): 857-870,
https://www.ncbi.nlm.nih.gov/pmc/articles/PMC5216096/; Nicole Lee,
"NASA's JPL Maneuvers a Robot Arm with Oculus Rift and Kinect 2,
Points to More Immersive Space Missions," *Engadget,* December 24, 2013,
https://www.engadget.com/2013-12-23-nasa-jpl-control-robotic-arm
-kinect-2.html.

30. "Azure Kinect DK," https://azure.microsoft.com/en-us/services/kinect
-dk/#overview.

31. NASA, "Global Positioning System History," October 27, 2012, last updated
August 7, 2017, https://www.nasa.gov/directorates/heo/scan/communications
/policy/GPS_History.html.

32. Wikipedia, s.v., "Inertial Navigation System," last modified January 20,
2022, https://en.wikipedia.org/wiki/Inertial_navigation_system#History.

33. Alex Woodie, "Big Growth Forecasted for Big Data, *Datanami,* January 22,
2022, https://www.datanami.com/2022/01/11/big-growth-forecasted
-for-big-data/.

34. Daniel Oberhaus, "NASA Is Training an AI to Detect Fresh Craters on
Mars," *Wired,* January 19, 2021, https://www.wired.com/story/nasa-is
-training-an-ai-to-detect-fresh-craters-on-mars/.

35. Seung Lee, "Microsoft, Alibaba AI Programs Beat Humans in a Stanford Reading Test," *Phys.org*, January 19, 2018, https://phys.org/news/2018-01-microsoft-alibaba-ai-humans-stanford.html.

36. Sherisse Pham, "Computers Are Getting Better at Reading than Humans," January 16, 2018, *CNN Money*, https://money.cnn.com/2018/01/15/technology/reading-robot-alibaba-microsoft-stanford/index.html.

37. Tom Simonite, "A Zelensky Deepfake Was Quickly Defeated: The Next One Might Not Be," *Wired*, March 17, 2022, https://www.wired.com/story/zelensky-deepfake-facebook-twitter-playbook/.

38. Olga Russakovsky, assistant professor of computer science, Princeton University, in conversation with Eric Niiler, June 4, 2021.

CHAPTER 2. SAVING LIVES WITH AI

1. Hyoyoung Jeong, Sung Soo Kwak, Seokwoo Sohn, John A. Rogers, et al., "Miniaturized Wireless, Skin-Integrated Sensor Networks for Quantifying Full-Body Movement Behaviors and Vital Signs in Infants," *PNAS* 118, no. 43 (October 18, 2021): e2104925118, https://doi.org/10.1073/pna.2104925118.

2. National Science Foundation, Information Technology Research Grant, R. Chellappa, University of Maryland, College Park, principal investigator, with T. Andriacchi, Stanford University, and C. Bregler, New York University, "New Technology for Capture, Analysis and Visualization of Human Movement Using Distributed Cameras," $2,560,000, September 15, 2003–September 14, 2009.

3. Nakano Nobuyasu, Sakura Tetsuro, Ueda Kazuhiro, et al., "Evaluation of 3D Markerless Motion Capture Accuracy Using OpenPose with Multiple Video Cameras," *Frontiers in Sports and Active Living* 2 (2020), https://doi.org/10.3389/fspor.2020.00050.

4. Robert Herpen, "Pose Estimation Provides Quick, Accurate Motion Tracking for Neuro Patients, *Healio News,* January 25, 2022, https://www.healio.com/news/neurology/20220125/pose-estimation-provides-quick-accurate-motion-tracking-for-neuro-patients; Joe Lemire, "Imagine

Carrying High-Grade Motion Capture and Biomechanical Analysis in Your Pocket: That's the Uplifting News from Uplift Labs," *Sports Techie,* January 25, 2022, https://www.sporttechie.com/imagine-carrying-high -grade-motion-capture-and-biomechanical-analysis-in-your-pocket-thats -the-uplifting-news-from-uplift-labs.

5. Ron Li, a physician and medical informatics director for Digital Health and AI Clinical Integration at Stanford Medicine, in conversation with Eric Niiler, July 26, 2021.

6. Pooja Rao, occupational therapist, Stanford Health Care, in conversation with Eric Niiler, August 4, 2021.

7. C. R. Manz, R. B. Parikh, D. S. Small, et al. "Effect of Integrating Machine Learning Mortality Estimates with Behavioral Nudges to Clinicians on Serious Illness Conversations among Patients with Cancer: A Stepped-Wedge Cluster Randomized Clinical Trial," *JAMA Oncology* 6, no. 12 (2020): e204759, https://doi.org/10.1001/jamaoncol.2020.4759.

8. Ravi Parikh, assistant professor of medical ethics and policy and medicine at the University of Pennsylvania, in conversation with Eric Niiler, August 3, 2021.

9. D. Ardila, A. P. Kiraly, S. Bharadwaj, et al., "End-to-End Lung Cancer Screening with Three-Dimensional Deep Learning on Low-Dose Chest Computed Tomography," *Nature Medicine* 25 (2019): 954–961, https://www .nature.com/articles/s41591-019-0447-x.

10. Casey Ross, "As the FDA Clears a Flood of AI Tools, Missing Data Raise Troubling Questions on Safety and Fairness," *STAT News*, Feb. 3, 2021, https://www.statnews.com/2021/02/03/fda-clearances-artificial -intelligence-data/.

11. Jeffrey Siewerdsen, professor of biomedical engineering, Johns Hopkins University, in conversation with Eric Niiler, August 5, 2021.

12. Z. D. Stephens, S. Y. Lee, F. Faghri, R. H. Campbell, C. Zhai, M. J. Efron, et al., "Big Data: Astronomical or Genomical?," *PLoS Biol* 13, no. 7 (2019): e1002195, https://doi.org/10.1371/journal.pbio.1002195.

13. HealthCare.gov, "Why Health Insurance Is Important: Protection from High Medical Costs," https://www.healthcare.gov/why-coverage-is -important/protection-from-high-medical-costs/; Sean P. Keehan, Gigi A. Cuckler, John A. Poisal, et al., "National Health Expenditure Projections, 2019–28: Expected Rebound in Prices Drives Rising Spending Growth," *Health Affairs* 39, no. 4 (2020): 704-714, https://www.healthaffairs .org/doi/full/10.1377/hlthaff.2020.00094?journalCode=hlthaff.

14. A. Kaushal, R. Altman, and C. Langlotz, "Geographic Distribution of US Cohorts Used to Train Deep Learning Algorithms," *JAMA* 324, no. 12 (2020): 1212–1213, doi:10.1001/jama.2020.12067.

15. Ziad Obermeyer, Brian Powers, Christine Vogeli, and Sendhil Mullainathan, "Dissecting Racial Bias in an Algorithm Used to Manage the Health of Populations," *Science* 366, no. 6464 (October 25, 2019): 447-453, https//doi.org/ 10.1126/science.aax2342.

16. Casey Ross, "From a Small Town in North Carolina to Big-City Hospitals: How Software Infuses Racism into U.S. Health Care," *Stat,* October 13, 2020, https://www.statnews.com/2020/10/13/how-software-infuses-racism -into-us-health-care/.

17. Boston Medical Center, "Framingham Study," https://www.bmc.org /stroke-and-cerebrovascular-center/research/framingham-study.

18. C. M. Gijsberts, K. A. Groenewegen, I. E. Hoefer, M. J. C. Eijkemans, F. W. Asselbergs, T. J. Anderson, et al., "Race/Ethnic Differences in the Associations of the Framingham Risk Factors with Carotid IMT and Cardiovascular Events," *PLoS ONE* 10, no. 7 (2015): e0132321, https://doi .org/10.1371/journal.pone.0132321.

19. S. Ahmed, C. T. Nutt, N. D. Eneanya, et al. "Examining the Potential Impact of Race Multiplier Utilization in Estimated Glomerular Filtration Rate Calculation on African-American Care Outcomes," *Journal of General Internal Medicine* 36 (2021): 464–471, https://doi.org/10.1007/s11606-020-06280-5.

20. Eric Niiler, "An AI Epidemiologist Sent the First Warnings of the Wuhan

Virus," *Wired*, January 25, 2020, https://www.wired.com/story/ai
-epidemiologist-wuhan-public-health-warnings/.

21. Justin Fendos, "How Surveillance Technology Powered South Korea's
COVID-19 Response," *Brooking Institution TechStream*, https://www
.brookings.edu/techstream/how-surveillance-technology-powered
-south-koreas-covid-19-response/.

22. S. Wongvibulsin, B. T. Garibaldi, A. A. R. Antar, et al., "Development of
Severe COVID-19 Adaptive Risk Predictor (SCARP): A Calculator to
Predict Severe Disease or Death in Hospitalized Patients with COVID-19,"
Annals of Internal Medicine 174, no. 6 (2021): 777-785, https://doi:10.7326/
M20-6754.

23. L. Wynants, B. Van Calster, G. S. Collins, R. D. Riley, G. Heinze, E. Schuit,
et al., "Prediction Models for Diagnosis and Prognosis of Covid-19:
Systematic Review and Critical Appraisal," *The BMJ* 369 (2020): m1328,
https://doi.org/10.1136/bmj.m1328.

24. M. Roberts, D. Driggs, M. Thorpe, et al., "Common Pitfalls and
Recommendations for Using Machine Learning to Detect and
Prognosticate for COVID-19 Using Chest Radiographs and CT Scans,"
Nature Machine Intelligence 3 (2021): 199–217, https://doi.org/10.1038
/s42256-021-00307-0.

25. Will Douglas Heaven, "Hundreds of AI Tools Have Been Built to Catch
Covid: None of Them Helped," *MIT Technology Review*, July 31, 2021,
https://www.technologyreview.com/2021/07/30/1030329
/machine-learning-ai-failed-covid-hospital-diagnosis-pandemic/.

26. Tom Simonite, "This AI Software Nearly Predicted Omicron's Tricky
Structure," *Wired*, January 18, 2022, https://www.wired.com/story/ai
-software-nearly-predicted-omicrons-tricky-structure/.

27. Katharine E. Henry, David N. Hager, Peter J. Pronovost, and Suchi Saria,
"A Targeted Real-Time Early Warning Score (Trewscore) for Septic Shock,"

Science Transactional Medicine 7, no. 299 (August 5, 2019): 299ra122, https://doi.org/10.1126/scitranslmed.aab3719.

28. Katharine E. Henry, Roy Adams, Cassandra Parent, Suchi Saria, et al., "Evaluating Adoption, Impact, and Factors Driving Adoption for TREWS, a Machine Learning–Based Sepsis Alerting System," *MedRxiv* (preprint), https://doi.org/10.1101/2021.07.02.21259941.

29. Elise Reuter, "Johns Hopkins Spinoff Building Risk Prediction Tools Emerges with $15M," *MedCityNews,* July 13, 2021, https://medcitynews.com/2021/07/johns-hopkins-spinoff-looking-to-build-better-risk-prediction-tools-emerges-with-15m/?rf=1; Melanie Blackman, "New Research-Backed Clinical AI Platform Launches," *HealthLeaders,* July 12, 2021, https://www.healthleadersmedia.com/technology/new-research-backed-clinical-ai-platform-launches.

30. Samuel G. Finlayson, Adarsh Subbaswamy, Karandeep Singh, et al., "Correspondence: The Clinician and Dataset Shift in Artificial Intelligence," *New England Journal of Medicine* 381 (July 15, 2021): 283-286, https://www.nejm.org/doi/full/10.1056/NEJMc2104626.

31. "Big Tech in Medicine: How Amazon, Apple, Microsoft, Google, IBM & NVIDIA Disrupt Healthcare," *The Medical Futurist,* August 24, 2021, https://medicalfuturist.com/tech-giants-in-healthcare-2021-summary/; Grand View Research, Market Analysis Report, "Artificial Intelligence in Healthcare Market Size, Share, and Trends Analysis Report by Component (Software Solutions, Hardware, Services), by Application (Virtual Assistants, Connected Machines), by Region, and Segment Forecasts, 2022–2030," January 2022, https://www.grandviewresearch.com/industry-analysis/artificial-intelligence-ai-healthcare-market.

32. Steve Lohr, "IBM Is Selling Off Watson Health to a Private Equity Firm," *New York Times,* January 21, 2022, https://www.nytimes.com/2022/01/21/business/ibm-watson-health.html.

CHAPTER 3: THE COMPLEXITIES AND CONTRIBUTIONS
OF FACIAL RECOGNITION

1. Clare Garvie, Alvara Bedoya, and Jonathan Frankel, "The Perpetual Line-Up: Unregulated Police Face Recognition in America," October 18, 2016, Georgetown Law, Center on Privacy and Technology, https://www.perpetuallineup.org/.

2. Kade Crockford, director, ACLU of Massachusetts Technology for Liberty Project, "How Is Face Recognition Surveillance Technology Racist?" *ACLU News and Commentary*, June 16, 2020, https://www.aclu.org/news/privacy-technology/how-is-face-recognition-surveillance-technology-racist/.

3. Joy Buolamwini and Timnit Gebru, "Gender Shades: Intersectional Accuracy Disparities in Commercial Gender Classification," *Proceedings of Machine Learning Research* 81 (2018): 1-15, http://proceedings.mlr.press/v81/buolamwini18a/buolamwini18a.pdf.

4. P. Jonathon Phillips, Amy N. Yaes, Ying Hu, Alice J. O'Toole, et al., "Face Recognition Accuracy of Forensic Examiners, Superrecognizers, and Face Recognition Algorithms," *PNAS* 115, no. 24 (May 29, 2018), https://doi.org/10.1073/pnas.1721355115.

5. Michael David Kelly, "Visual Identification of People by Computer" (PhD thesis, Stanford University, Department of Computer Science, 1970).

6. Takeo Kanade, *Computer Recognition of Human Faces* (Basel and Stuttgart: Birkhauser Verlag, 1977), http://citeseerx.ist.psu.edu/viewdoc/download?doi=10.1.1.448.2368&rep=rep1&type=pdf.

7. Ken Klippenstein and Sara Sirota, "The Taliban Have Seized US Military Biometrics Devices," *The Intercept*, August 17, 2021, https://theintercept.com/2021/08/17/afghanistan-taliban-military-biometrics/.

8. Dana Canedy, "Tampa Scans the Faces in Its Crowds for Criminals," *New York Times*, July 4, 2001, https://www.nytimes.com/2001/07/04/us/tampa-scans-the-faces-in-its-crowds-for-criminals.html.

9. Y. LeCun, B. Boser, J. S. Denker, D. Henderson, R. E. Howard, W. Hubbard,

and L. D. Jackel, "Handwritten Digit Recognition with a Back-Propagation Network," in David Touretzky, ed., *Advances in Neural Information Processing Systems 2 (NIPS 1989)*, https://proceedings.neurips.cc/paper/1989/file/53c3bce66e43be4f209556518c2fcb54-Paper.pdf.

10. Alex Krizhevsky, Ilya Sutskever, and Geoffrey E. Hinton, "ImageNet Classification with Deep Convolutional Neural Networks," *Communications of the ACM* 60 (6) (2017): 84–90, https://doi.org/10.1145/3065386.

11. Eric Hofesmann, "Google's Open Images Now Easier to Download and Evaluate with FiftyOne," *Toward Data Science,* May 12, 2021, https://towardsdatascience.com/googles-open-images-now-easier-to-download-and-evaluate-with-fiftyone-615ce0482c02.

12. Lauren Goode, "Facial Recognition Software Is Biased towards White Men, Researcher Finds," *The Verge,* February 11, 2018.

13. Steve Lohr, "Facial Recognition Is Accurate, If You're a White Guy," *New York Times,* February 9, 2018, https://www.nytimes.com/2018/02/09/technology/facial-recognition-race-artificial-intelligence.html.

14. Morgan Klaus Scheuerman, Jacob M. Paul, and Jed R. Brubaker, "How Computers See Gender: An Evaluation of Gender Classification in Commercial Facial Analysis Services," *Proceedings of the ACM on Human-Computer Interaction* 3 (CSCW), article 144 (November 2019): 1-33, https://doi.org/10.1145/3359246.

15. Bobby Allyn, "IBM Abandons Facial Recognition Products, Condemns Racially Biased Surveillance," *NPR.org,* June 9, 2020, https://www.npr.org/2020/06/09/873298837/ibm-abandons-facial-recognition-products-condemns-racially-biased-surveillance.

16. Drew Harwell, "Federal Study Confirms Racial Bias of Many Facial-Recognition Systems, Casts Doubt on Their Expanding Use," *Washington Post,* December 19, 2019, https://www.washingtonpost.com/technology/2019/12/19/federal-study-confirms-racial-bias-many-facial-recognition-systems-casts-doubt-their-expanding-use/.

17. Kashmir Hill, "Another Arrest, and Jail Time, Due to Bad Facial Recognition Match," *New York Times*, December 29, 2020, https://www.nytimes .com/2020/12/29/technology/facial-recognition-misidentify-jail.html.

18. Government Accountability Office, *Facial Recognition Technology: Current and Planned Uses by Federal Agencies,* GAO 21-526 (August 24, 2021), https:// www.gao.gov/products/gao-21-526.

19. Patrick Grother, Austin Hom, Mei Nagan, and Kayee Hanaoka, "Facial Recognition Vendor Test, Part 7: Identification for Paperless Travel and Immigration," NISTIR 8381, https://doi.org/10.6028/NIST.IR.8381.

20. Matthew Kay, Cynthia Matuszek, and Sean A. Munson, "Unequal Representation and Gender Stereotypes in Image Search Results for Occupations," *Proceedings of the 33rd Annual ACM Conference on Human Factors in Computing Systems* (April 2015): 3819–3828, https://doi. org/10.1145/2702123.2702520.

21. Charles Isbell, dean of computing, Georgia Institute of Technology, in conversation with Eric Niiler, July 8, 2021.

22. Office of US Representative Pramila Jayapal, "Jayapal and Lawmakers Introduce Bicameral Legislation to Ban the Use of Facial Recognition Technology by the Government," news release, June 15, 2021, https: //jayapal.house.gov/2021/06/15/ban-facial-recognition-tech/.

23. Khari Johnson, "Alondra Nelson Wants to Make Science and Tech More Just," *Wired,* June 29, 2021, https://www.wired.com/story/alondra -nelson-make-science-tech-more-just/.

24. Office of Science and Technology Policy, "Notice of Request for Information (RFI) on Public and Private Sector Uses of Biometric Technologies," *Federal Register* 86, no. 193 (October 8, 2021): 56300-56302, https://www.govinfo.gov/content/pkg/FR-2021-10-08/html/2021-21975. htm.

25. Maryland State Senator Charles Sydnor in conversation with Eric Niiler, August 18, 2021,

26. James Vincent, "FBI Used Facial Recognition to Identify a Capitol Rioter from His Girlfriend's Instagram Posts," *The Verge,* April 21, 2021, https://www.theverge.com/2021/4/21/22395323/fbi-facial-recognition-us-capital-riots-tracked-down-suspect.

27. Kashmir Hill, "The Facial-Recognition App Clearview Sees a Spike in Use after Capitol Attack," *New York Times,* January 9, 2021, https://www.nytimes.com/2021/01/09/technology/facial-recognition-clearview-capitol.html.

28. Rachel Metz, "Clearview AI Sued in California by Immigrant Rights Groups, Activists," *CNN.com,* March 9, 2021, https://www.cnn.com/2021/03/09/tech/clearview-ai-mijente-lawsuit/index.html.

29. Matt O'Brien and Tali Arbel, "Illinois Lawsuit against Clearview AI Discloses Future Commercial Plans for Controversial Privacy Practices," *Chicago Journal,* April 2, 2022, https://www.chicagojournal.com/illinois-lawsuit-against-clearview-ai-discloses-future-commercial-plans-for-controversial-privacy-practices/.

30. Federal Bureau of Investigation, "Most Wanted: Capitol Violence," https://www.fbi.gov/wanted/capitol-violence.

31. Tom Simonite, "How Facial Recognition Is Fighting Child Sex Trafficking," *Wired,* June 19, 2019, https://www.wired.com/story/how-facial-recognition-fighting-child-sex-trafficking/.

32. Francesca Street, "How Facial Recognition Is Taking Over Airports," *CNN.com,* October 8, 2019, https://www.cnn.com/travel/article/airports-facial-recognition/index.html.

33. US Customs and Border Protection, "ORD and MDW Encourages Travelers to Use Facial Recognition," news release, August 2, 2021, https://www.cbp.gov/newsroom/local-media-release/ord-and-mdw-encourages-travelers-use-facial-recognition; US Customs and Border Protection, "CBP at MSP Encourages Travelers to Use Facial Recognition," news release, August 24, 2021, https://www.cbp.gov/newsroom/local-media-release/cbp-msp-encourages-travelers-use-facial-recognition.

34. Elaine Glusac, "Your Face Is, or Will Be, Your Boarding Pass," *New York Times,* December 7, 2021, https://www.nytimes.com/2021/12/07/travel /biometrics-airports-security.html.

35. P. J. Griekspoor, "Artificial Intelligence Can Track Cattle in Database by Recognizing Their Faces," *Farm Progress,* October 14, 2020, https://www.farmprogress.com/livestock/cows-have-individual-faces-can -be-traced-facial-recognition.

36. A. Kale et al., "Identification of Humans Using Gait," *IEEE Transactions on Image Processing* 13 (2004): 1163-1173, https://doi.org/10.1109/TIP.2004.832865.

CHAPTER FOUR: THE PROMISE OF AUTONOMOUS VEHICLES

1. Ernst Dickmanns, in an oral history conducted in 2010 by Peter Asaro, Indiana University, Bloomington Indiana, for Indiana University and the IEEE, https://ethw.org/Oral-History:Ernst_Dickmanns#Robotic_Vision _Systems_for_Automobiles.

2. Janosch Delcker, "The Man Who Invented the Self-Driving Car (in 1986)," *Politico,* July 19, 2018, https://www.politico.eu/article/delf-driving -car-born-1986-ernst-dickmanns-mercedes/.

3. Delcker, "The Man Who Invented the Self-Driving Car."

4. Lockheed Martin, "Driving Forces: Autonomous Land Vehicles," https:// www.lockheedmartin.com/en-us/news/features/history/alv.html.

5. Lockheed Martin, "Driving Forces."

6. Chuck Thorpe, professor of computer science, Clarkson University, in conversation with Eric Niiler, October 6, 2021.

7. Nita Congress, "The Automated Highway System: An Idea Whose Time Has Come," *Public Roads* 58, no. 1 (Summer 1994), https://highways.dot.gov/public -roads/summer-1994/automated-highway-system-idea-whose-time-has-come.

8. Mike Pesarchick, "When Self-Driving Tech Was New, a Road Trip Paved the Way," Associated Press, August 11, 2020, https://apnews.com/article /pittsburgh-plays-7eaf98e853534958a422ec71e100c4c0.

9. Robotics Institute, Carnegie Mellon University, "Navlab: The Carnegie Mellon University Navigation Laboratory," https://www.cs.cmu.edu/afs/cs/project/alv/www/.

10. Carnegie Mellon University, "Road Infrastructure: Inventory and Assessment," http://www.cs.cmu.edu/~road/.

11. "How Pittsburgh Is Test Driving Tech to Make Your Commute Smarter," PBS NewsHour, September 6, 2017, https://www.pbs.org/newshour/show/pittsburgh-test-driving-tech-make-commute-smarter.

12. Bruce F. Field and Charles Fenimore, *Video Processing with the Princeton Engine at NIST,* NIST Technical Note 1288 (Washington, DC: US Department of Commerce, National Institute of Standards and Technology, 1991), https://www.govinfo.gov/content/pkg/GOVPUB-C13-64a7ae8f5e207d30fb18e14bb9f82373/pdf.

13. Douglas W. Gage, "A Brief History of Unmanned Ground Vehicle (UGV) Development Efforts," *Unmanned Systems Magazine* 13, no. 3 (Summer 1995): 1-9, https://apps.dtic.mil/sti/pdfs/ADA422845.pdf.

14. Defense Advanced Research Projects Agency, *UAVs,* https://www.darpa.mil/about-us/timeline/amber-predator-global-hawk-predator.

15. Thomas Strat, president and CEO, DZYNE Technologies, in conversation with Eric Niiler, October 7, 2021.

16. "The Great Robot Race," NOVA, March 28, 2006, https://www.pbs.org/wgbh/nova/darpa/.

17. Joseph Hooper, "From DARPA Grand Challenge, 2004: DARPA's Debacle in the Desert," *Popular Science,* June 4, 2004, https://www.popsci.com/scitech/article/2004-06/darpa-grand-challenge-2004darpas-debacle-desert/.

18. Hooper, "From DARPA Grand Challenge, 2004."

19. Phil LeBeau, "Autonomous Driving Start-Up Aurora Plans to Go Public through SPAC Deal with Initial Value of $11 billion," *CNBC,* July 15, 2021, https://www.cnbc.com/2021/07/15/autonomous-driving-start-up-aurora-plans-to-go-public-through-spac-deal-.html.

20. Chris Urmson, CEO, Aurora, in conversation with Eric Niiler, August 22, 2021.

21. Kirsten Korosec, "Aurora Shines Spotlight on Autonomous Truck Tech, Strategy Ahead of SPAC Merger," *TechCrunch+*, September 30, 2021, https://techcrunch.com/2021/09/30/aurora-shines-spotlight-on-autonomous-truck-tech-strategy-ahead-of-spac-merger/.

22. Danielle Muoio, "Ranked: The 18 Companies Most Likely to Get Self-Driving Cars on the Road First," *Business Insider,* September 27, 2017, https://www.businessinsider.com/the-companies-most-likely-to-get-driverless-cars-on-the-road-first-2017-4.

23. US Department of Transportation, National Highway Safety Administration, ODI Résumé, Investigation PE 21-020, opened August 13, 2021, https://static.nhtsa.gov/odi/inv/2021/INOA-PE21020-1893.PDF.

24. Michael Butler, "Tesla Driver Crashes into Cop Car while Watching Movie," *Motortrend Carbuzz,* August 27, 2020, https://carbuzz.com/news/tesla-driver-crashes-into-cop-car-while-watching-movie.

25. A. Kierstein, "Feds Open Probe of 765,000 Tesla Vehicles over Autopilot Crashes," *Motortrend News,* August 16, 2021, https://www.motortrend.com/news/nhtsa-tesla-autopilot-fsd-crash-investigation/.

26. Faiz Siddiqui and Jeremy B. Merrill, "Tesla 'Phantom Braking' Issue Is Focus of Federal Safety Probe after Owners Bombard Government Website with Complaints," *Washington Post,* February 17, 2022, https://www.washingtonpost.com/technology/2022/02/17/tesla-phantom-braking/.

27. Neal E. Boudette, "Tesla's Autopilot Technology Faces Fresh Scrutiny," *New York Times,* March 23, 2021, updated September 1, 2021, https://www.nytimes.com/2021/03/23/business/teslas-autopilot-safety-investigations.html.

28. "Uber's Self-Driving Operator Charged over Fatal Crash," *BBC News,* September 16, 2020, https://www.bbc.com/news/technology-54175359.

29. Missy Cummings, professor of electrical and computer engineering, Duke

University, and director of the Humans and Autonomy Laboratory and
Duke Robotics, in conversation with Eric Niiler, September 23, 2021.

30. Alberto Morando, Pnina Gershon, Bruce Mehler, and Bryan Reimer,
"A Model for Naturalistic Glance Behavior around Tesla Autopilot
Disengagements," *Accident Analysis & Prevention* 161 (October 2021):
106348, https://doi.org/10.1016/j.aap.2021.106348.

31. Tesla Support, "Full Self-Driving Computer Installations," https://www
.tesla.com/support/full-self-driving-computer.

32. Maija Palmer, "Driverless Cars to Arrive on European Streets Next Year,"
Sifted, September 7, 2021, https://sifted.eu/articles/driverless-cars-europe-vay.

33. "On the Future of Our Roads: Cathy Wu," *Robot Brains* podcast, season 2,
episode 6, https://www.therobotbrains.ai/who-is-cathy-wu-mit.

34. Cathy Wu, Abdul Rahman Kreidieh, Kanaad Parvate, Eugene Vinitsky, and
Alexandre M. Bayen, "Flow: A Modular Learning Framework for Mixed
Autonomy Traffic," *IEEE Transactions on Robotics,* July 16, 2021, https:
//doi.org/10.1109/TRO.2021.3087314.

CHAPTER FIVE: AI'S FUTURESCAPE

1. Amanda Zrebiec, "Pedro Rodriguez: Natural Intelligence," Johns Hopkins
Applied Physics Laboratory, April 27, 2021, https://www.jhuapl.edu
/FeatureStory/210427-Pedro-Rodriguez-humanitarian-assistance-disaster
-recovery-AI.

2. Eric Niiler, "As the Arctic Warms, AI Forecasts Scope Out Shifting Sea
Ice," *Wired,* November 3, 2021, https://www.wired.com/story/as-the
-arctic-warms-ai-forecasts-scope-out-shifting-sea-ice.

3. Tongshu Zheng, Michael H. Bergin, Shijia Hu, Joshua Miller, and David E.
Carlson, "Estimating Ground-Level PM2.5 Using Micro-Satellite Images
by a Convolutional Neural Network and Random Forest Approach,"
Atmospheric Environment 230 (June 1, 2020): 117451, https://doi
.org/10.1016/j.atmosenv.2020.117451.

4. US Environmental Protection Agency, "U.S. Government Global Methane Initiative Accomplishments," https://www.epa.gov/gmi/importance -methane.

5. David Rolnick, Priya L. Donti, Lynn H. Kaack, Kelly Kochanski, et al., "Tackling Climate Change with Machine Learning," *ACM Computing Surveys* 55, no. 2 (February 7, 2022): 1-96, https://doi.org/10.1145/3485128.

6. Frances Robles, "Months After Puerto Rico Earthquakes, Thousands Are Still Living Outside," *New York Times,* March 1, 2020, https://www.nytimes .com/2020/03/01/us/puerto-rico-earthquakes-fema.html.

7. Zrebiec, "Pedro Rodriguez."

8. Eric Rignot, professor of earth system science, University of California, Irvine, in conversation with Eric Niiler, October 28, 2021.

9. Pedro Rodriguez, Senior Technical Leader, Johns Hopkins University Applied Physics Laboratory, in conversation with Eric Niiler, October 26, 2021.

10. American Astronomical Society, "AAS Members Share 2020 Viktor Ambartsumian Prize," July 20, 2020, https://aas.org/posts/news/2020/07 /aas-members-share-2020-viktor-ambartsumian-prize.

11. Alex Szalay, Bloomberg Distinguished Professor of Physics and Astronomy and Computer Science, Johns Hopkins University School of Arts and Sciences and Whiting School of Engineering, in conversation with Eric Niiler, October 25, 2021.

12. European Space Agency, "Gaia: ESA's Billion Star Surveyor," https://www .esa.int/Science_Exploration/Space_Science/Gaia.

13. US Social Security Admin., Actuarial Publications: Cohort Life Expectancy, Table TV.A4, https://www.ssa.gov/oact/TR/2011/lr5a4.html#foot2.

14. US Census Bureau, "Older People Projected to Outnumber Children for First Time in U.S. History," Release CB18-41, March 13, 2018, https://www .census.gov/newsroom/press-releases/2018/cb18-41-population-projections. html.

15. H. Ding, S. K. Zhou, and R. Chellappa, "FaceNet2ExpNet: Regularizing a Deep Face Recognition Net for Expression Recognition," *12th IEEE International Conference on Automatic Face & Gesture Recognition (FG 2017)* (2017): 118-126, https://doi.org/10.1109/FG.2017.23.

16. S. Taheri, Q. Qiu, and R. Chellappa, "Structure-Preserving Sparse Decomposition for Facial Expression Analysis," *IEEE Transactions on Image Processing* 23, no. 8 (August 2014): 3590-3603, https://doi.org/10.1109/TIP.2014.2331141.

17. Mohammad Rafayet Ali, Taylor Myers, Ellen Wagner, Harshil Ratnu, E. Ray Dorsey, and Ehsan Hoque, "Facial Expressions Can Detect Parkinson's Disease: Preliminary Evidence from Videos Collected Online," *NPJ Digital Medicine* 4, article 129 (2021), https://doi.org/10.1038/s41746-021-00502-8.

18. Laureano Moro-Velázquez, Jorge Andrés Gómez-García, Juan Ignacio Godino-Llorente, Jesús Villalba, Juan Rafael Orozco-Arroyave, and Najim Dehak, "Analysis of Speaker Recognition Methodologies and the Influence of Kinetic Changes to Automatically Detect Parkinson's Disease," *Applied Soft Computing* 62 (2018): 649-666, https://doi.org/10.1016/j.asoc.2017.11.001.

19. Raghavendra Pappagari, Jaejin Cho, Laureano Moro-Velázquez, Najim Dehak, "Using State-of-the-Art Speaker Recognition and Natural Language Processing Technologies to Detect Alzheimer's Disease and Assess Its Severity," *Proceedings Interspeech 2020*: 2177-2181, https://doi.org/10.21437/Interspeech.2020-2587; R. Pappagari, T. Wang, J. Villalba, N. Chen, and N. Dehak, "X-Vectors Meet Emotions: A Study on Dependencies between Emotion and Speaker Recognition," *2020 IEEE International Conference on Acoustics, Speech and Signal Processing (ICASSP)*: 7169-7173, https://doi.org/10.1109/ICASSP40776.2020.9054317.

20. Molly Price, "Amazon Launches Alexa Together Caregiver Subscription on Echo Devices," *CNet,* December 10, 2021, https://www.cnet.com/home/amazon-launches-alexa-together-caregiver-subscription-on-echo-devices/.

21. Amazon, Echo Show 5 (2nd Gen, 2021 release), Smart display with Alexa and 2 MP camera, Glacier White, https://www.amazon.com/Echo-Show -5-2nd-Gen-2021-release/dp/B08J8H8L5T.

22. S. Gerke, C. Shachar, P. R. Chai, et al. "Regulatory, Safety, and Privacy Concerns of Home Monitoring Technologies during COVID-19," *Nature Medicine* 26 (2020): 1176-1182, https://doi.org/10.1038/s41591-020-0994-1.

23. D. Dakopoulos and N. G. Bourbakis, "Wearable Obstacle Avoidance Electronic Travel Aids for the Blind: A Survey," *IEEE Transactions on Systems, Man, and Cybernetics, Part C (Applications and Reviews)* 40, no. 1 (January 2020): 25-35, https://doi.org/10.1109/TSMCC.2009.2021255.

24. Cara LaPointe, codirector, Johns Hopkins Institute for Assured Autonomy, in conversation with Eric Niiler, October 6, 2021.

25. Mark MacCarthy and Kenneth Propp, "Machines Learn That Brussels Writes the Rules: The EU's New AI Regulation," May 4, 2021, Brookings Institution blog, https://www.brookings.edu/blog/techtank/2021/05/04 /machines-learn-that-brussels-writes-the-rules-the-eus-new-ai-regulation/.

26. The White House, "The Biden Administration Launches the National Artificial Intelligence Research Resource Task Force," Press Release, June 10, 2021, https://www.whitehouse.gov/ostp/news-updates/2021/06/10. /the-biden-administration-launches-the-national-artificial-intelligence -research-resource-task-force/.

27. Jennifer Conrad and Will Knight, "China Is About to Regulate AI—and the World Is Watching," *Wired,* February 22, 2022, https://www.wired.com /story/china-regulate-ai-world-watching/#intcid=_wired-verso-hp -trending_0427e12a-a3d1-448f-9e66-6046ea2a0e78_popular4-1.

28. Reuters, "Pentagon Explores a New Frontier in the World of Virtual Intelligence," *New York Times,* May 30, 2003, https://www.nytimes.com /2003/05/30/us/pentagon-explores-a-new-frontier-in-the-world-of -virtual-intelligencehtml?src=pm&gwh=C39232292790FE3ED00 B94B118A98CA1&gwt=pay.

29. "Pentagon Kills LifeLog Project," *Wired*, February 4, 2004, https://www
.wired.com/2004/02/pentagon-kills-lifelog-project/.

30. Muhammad Afzaal, "Explainable AI for Data-Driven Feedback and
Intelligent Action Recommendations to Support Student Self-Regulation,"
Frontiers in Artificial Intelligence, November 12, 2021, https://doi.org
/10.3389/frai.2021.723447.

31. Defense Advanced Research Projects Agency, "DARPA Announces
Research Teams Selected to Semantic Forensics Program," news release,
March 2, 2021, https://www.darpa.mil/news-events/2021-03-02; Defense
Advanced Research Projects Agency, "DARPA Open Sources Resources to
Aid Evaluation of Adversarial AI Defenses," news release, December 21,
2021, https://www.darpa.mil/news-events/2021-12-21.

Index

inertial measurement units (IMUs), 28–29

infrared cameras, 28, 103, 105

Institute for Data Intensive Engineering and Science (IDEIS), 134–35

Institute of Automation of the Chinese Academy of Sciences, 74

Intel, 95, 112

intellectual property, 80–83

Intelligent Vehicle Highway System, 101

iris recognition, 70–72

Isbell, Charles, 3, 84–85

IUBA (Image Understanding for Battlefield Awareness), 105, xv–xvi

January 6, 2021, insurrection, 9, 87–88, 110

JANUS-, 75, 77, 81, xix

Kanade, Takeo, 67

Kashyap, R. L., xiii

Kasparaov, Gary, 26

Kelly, Michael David, 66–67

kidney patients, 50–51

Kinect, 27–28, 144

Kitty Hawk Corporation, 113

Kriegman, David, 67

Krizhevsky, Alex, 25, 74

LADAR (laser detection and ranging), 27, 103, 104

lane change warnings, 28, 97, 121

lane identification, 96

language processing and translating, 30–31, 142, 160

LaPointe, Cara, 145–46

law enforcement: and facial recognition, 9–10, 63, 68–69, 77, 86–89, 90–91, xix, xvii; and predictive policing, 7–8; regulations on use of AI, 77, 86–89, 147, 149; uses, 7–9, xvii

Learned-Miller, Erik, 74

LeCun, Yann, 73

Li, Ron, 39–40

LIDAR (light detection and ranging), 115

LifeLog, 151–52, 153

light: and AVs, 99; and facial recognition, 65; and night-vision cameras, 28; and sensor challenges, 7

Lighthill, James, xvi

loss, face detection, 83

loss, pose estimation, 83

lung cancer, 43–44

machine learning: child-machine model, 3, 14; and data shift issue, 61; and data size, 11; defined, 10–11, 160; development of, 25; and generalization, 38, 60; and patient